# GENERATIVE AI BASICS & BEYOND

LEARN EFFECTIVE PROMPT ENGINEERING QUICKLY & EASILY TO HARNESS THE POWER OF TOOLS LIKE CHATGPT FOR PRODUCTIVITY, CAREER SUCCESS, & CREATIVITY—EVEN IF YOU'RE A BEGINNER

MELISSA PENEYCAD

***To the innovators, the skeptics, and the endlessly curious.***

*To those who see AI not as a replacement for human creativity but as a collaborator in the grand act of imagination.*

***To my family—who have caught every curveball, cheered for every wild idea, and given me both the wings to explore and the roots to return.***

*To the artists, the thinkers, the problem-solvers, and the dreamers who dare to explore new frontiers—may this book empower you to harness the extraordinary without losing sight of what makes us profoundly human.*

***To the early readers and reviewers, your thoughtful insights, encouragement, and honest critiques helped shape this book into something far better than I could have done alone.***

*And finally, to the AI tools that lent a digital hand in creating this book—your tireless, algorithmic efforts are appreciated (but let's not get any ideas about taking credit).*

# INTRODUCTION

It's 7:30 AM when you enter your office, a cup of coffee in hand, ready to start your day. You got to work early to catch up on email, read a lengthy report, and edit an article due by 10:00 AM. Even though you're an hour and a half early, your colleague Aiden is already there and has, in fact, been there all night. However, Aiden isn't a person and does not need a cup of coffee to feel energized in the morning. Instead, it's an AI that crafts reports, designs presentations, brainstorms ideas, summarizes long reports, and more. This AI is new to you, so you have not realized its full potential, but you are excited about the possibilities when suddenly it dawns on you that you can get Aiden to write your emails for you, summarize the report so you don't have to read it cover to cover, and even edit your article!

So, as you hand over these tasks to Aiden, you find yourself with plenty of time to spare. You decide that tomorrow, you will come to work on time instead of an hour and a half early, allowing you to sleep a little longer or spend more time with your family in the morning. This might sound like a dream, but it's real and happening right now in offices across the globe.

### *Why is learning about generative AI important?*

During a fireside talk at Stanford Graduate School of Business in 2017, Dr. Andrew Ng—then VP and Chief Scientist of Baidu but perhaps best known for co-founding Coursera—compared AI to electricity. He said:

> *Just as electricity transformed almost everything 100 years ago, today I actually have a hard time thinking of an industry that I don't think AI will transform in the next several years.*

Ng was spot-on; AI now touches nearly every aspect of our lives. In recent years, generative AI use has skyrocketed thanks to its broad applicability, personalization capabilities, interactivity, accessibility, and user-friendliness. This rapid expansion may feel overwhelming, but if you look around, it is starting to resemble how smartphones and the internet have become indispensable parts of everyday life.

That's why I argue that in today's fast-paced world, understanding generative AI isn't a luxury; for many of us, knowing how to effectively use this technology is increasingly necessary. Hadi Partovi, entrepreneur, investor, and CEO of Code.org, put it best when he stated:

> *When people think about job losses due to AI, the risk isn't people losing their jobs to AI... it's losing their job to somebody else who knows how to use AI.*

I understand entirely if you're nervous about AI and its rapid pace of advancement. Experts often highlight the importance of placing guardrails around AI's development, ensuring it benefits society without introducing unnecessary risks. These are some of the themes we'll explore later in this book. Regardless of how you feel about AI in general—and generative AI in particular—this technology is here to stay. After all, the internet wasn't a passing phase, and neither is AI. Here's what Yann LeCun, a Turing Award-winning artificial intelligence researcher who serves as Chief AI Scientist at Meta, said at the World Economic Forum:

> *The...thing that everybody is talking about is generative AI... This is going to make people more creative. Those systems will understand the physical world. They will be able to remember and...reason and plan.*

Generative AI can be a substantial asset for many people: professionals looking to boost productivity, students seeking extra support, job seekers hoping to stand out, entrepreneurs striving for innovation, and artists and writers craving fresh ideas. This book will discuss the many positives of generative AI; however, providing a balanced perspective on this technology is extremely important to me, so it will also focus on its risks and challenges. Ultimately, I aim to offer guidance on using AI responsibly rather than avoiding it out of fear.

You might assume AI is a dry, overly technical, or intimidating subject. While there are many technical aspects to it—and we will get into some of them in subsequent chapters—when it comes to learning generative AI, the experience is anything but dull! I believe you will find exploring this technology to be surprisingly engaging and fun, thanks to its creative and visual nature, customizability, and ability to yield immediate, often fascinating results. Along the way, you will see how mastering generative AI does not require a computer science degree; rather, a healthy dose of curiosity and a willingness to explore and learn is the essence of what's required.

Throughout this book, I will show you practical ways to harness the power of AI in your personal and professional life. This will equip you to adapt to the fast pace of change and ensure that AI remains a helpful ally rather than an intimidating adversary.

### *What is the purpose of this book?*

This book aims to guide you through the exciting world of generative AI. Whether you're just starting your journey with AI or are already on your way, this book offers something for you. My goals for this book are fourfold: First, to explain generative AI in easy-to-understand terms. Second, to demonstrate the breadth of industries and sectors benefiting from this technology, without using the same, overused examples you will find in other books. Third, to provide a balanced perspective of this technology by exploring both its pitfalls and potential. And finally, to inspire you to continue to explore generative AI's potential in your personal and professional life.

### *How is this book structured?*

First things first, this is not a textbook, but you will undoubtedly learn a lot by reading its pages. Instead, this book has been designed to guide you through generative AI in a clear, accessible, and engaging manner, starting with the basics and moving beyond them to more advanced topics, all while staying within reach of those new to this field. Foundational topics such as neural networks, large language models, and prompt engineering—the art and science of crafting effective inputs to achieve optimal AI responses—will be explored in sufficient detail without being overwhelming. It also includes ample examples and hands-on activities to reinforce learning and practical engagement with generative AI.

Each chapter includes QR codes you can scan with your smartphone for quick access to digital content, including:

- *end-of-chapter quizzes* to reinforce learning,
- *bonus chapters* that expand on key topics, and
- *step-by-step tutorials* for hands-on practice with generative AI.

Short and intuitive URLs are also provided for those who prefer using a computer.

While many will read this book cover to cover, I recognize that interests, experience levels, and learning goals vary. To accommodate a broad audience, I have designed five personalized learning tracks (outlined in Table 1).

## Table 1: Five learning tracks

| Learning Track | This track is ideal if... | Essential chapters | Recommended chapters | Optional chapters |
|---|---|---|---|---|
| 1. The essentials | ...you are a beginner, looking for a place to begin exploring generative AI. | 1, 2, 3, 4 (pt. 1) | 5, 8, 9, 10, 11 | 12, 13, 14, and Bonus Chapters 1, 2, 3 |
| 2. Beyond the basics | ...you have some experience in generative AI and are looking to move beyond the basics. | chapter 4—especially pt. 2, 7, 11, 13, 14 | 1, 2, 3, 4, 5, 8, 9, 10 | 6, 12, and Bonus Chapters 1, 2 3 |
| 3. Practical applications | ...you are interested in gaining direct experience using AI tools (beginners and those with more experience). | 1, 2, 3, 4, 5, 7, 10, 11 | 8, 9, 12, 13 | 6, 14, and Bonus Chapters 1, 2, 3 |
| 4. Career advancement | ...you are looking to use generative AI in your work or pivot into a new role more focused on AI. | 4, 7, 10, 11, 14, Bonus Chapters 1, 2, and 3 | 1, 2, 3, 8, 12, 13 | 5, 6, 9 |
| 5. History, ethics, and trends | ...if you are primarily interested in the history and ethics of generative AI and want insight into the future. | 1, 5, 6, 8, 12, 13, | 2, 3, 4, 9, 14 | 7, 10, 11, Bonus Chapters 1, 2, 3 |

### *What will you get out of this book?*

If you actively engage with the material in this book, I'm confident you will gain valuable skills and insights that extend far beyond the pages. You will build practical skills that translate to real-world use, whether starting from scratch or already exploring AI. Along the way, you will develop a deeper understanding of generative AI, uncovering its immense potential while recognizing its challenges and limitations. With a strong foundation, you will be equipped to progress from beginner to proficient user, refining your abilities and advancing quickly.

Beyond technical skills, this book emphasizes the critical role of human oversight in AI, showing how creativity, ethics, and regulation shape responsible AI use and development. You will also learn how to navigate a digital-first world safely, distinguishing AI-generated content from reality, separating fact from fiction, and protecting yourself from scams and misinformation. Finally, you will reinforce your learning and build confidence through hands-on activities and end-of-chapter quizzes.

### ***Who am I? And how was this book created?***

The second question kicking off this section might seem curious, but I promise it will become clear. Before we get to that, allow me the opportunity to introduce myself. After all, we are about to embark on an exciting journey together, and it is only fair that you know your guide.

**Left:** Author speaking on AI in infrastructure and public-private partnerships at a UNECE event, Geneva, Nov. 2024. **Right:** Author discussing AI in communications at the AI in Regulation Conference, Toronto, Feb. 2025. Photos courtesy of Daniel Roukema, MDR Strategy Group.

I am the author of the Amazon bestselling book *Essentials of AI for Beginners,* which introduced many readers—perhaps even you!—to the transformative potential of artificial intelligence. I have had the great honor and privilege of sharing my perspective on AI at events hosted by the United Nations Economic Commission for Europe (UNECE) in Geneva, Switzerland and at a pioneering conference on AI in regulation in Toronto, Canada alongside local and global leaders.

As a lifelong learner, I thrive on discovering innovative ways to tackle challenges and embrace new possibilities. Artificial intelligence has been a transformative tool in my journey, empowering me to quickly and cost-effectively learn new skills, elevate the quality of my work, and regain valuable time for hobbies, travel, and family.

Generative AI, in particular, has been a game-changer—and I'm confident it can be for you, too.

Although I do not have a formal computer programming or data science background, I excel as a communicator—a vital skill in generative AI, as you will see throughout this book. Furthermore, I've always had a technical mind, naturally drawn to fields such as engineering and environmental sustainability.

I eagerly embrace emerging technologies in my personal and professional life, bring entrepreneurial experience to the table, and use my critical and out-of-the-box thinking skills to design and implement innovative tools, frameworks, and systems for my clients. In addition, creativity is central to who I am, whether painting, writing, designing my home, or throwing clay.

Therefore, my diverse skills, interests, and experiences—combined with my blend of technical expertise and creative curiosity—made generative AI a natural fit for me. It bridges the analytical and the imaginative, offering endless possibilities for crafting, innovating, and problem-solving. Whether brainstorming ideas, designing projects, or streamlining processes, I have seen firsthand how AI can amplify human potential, including my own.

My AI journey has been driven by curiosity, creativity, and practicality. These qualities shape how I approach this technology and consider how it influences how we work, think, and create.

With a solid foundation in AI, diverse practical experience, and a unique mix of expertise and insight, I believe I'm well-positioned to guide you through this transformative technology. Together, we'll explore its possibilities and learn how to use it to achieve your goals.

Now, let's tackle the second question: *How was this book created?* Given that this is a book on generative AI, it's a fair question! I believe in full transparency, so I want to be clear—AI assisted me in various ways throughout the writing process, but AI did not write this book. Every passage in every chapter is my own, reflecting my voice, insights, and expertise. My role wasn't just to oversee AI-generated content but to craft, refine, and ensure that every word aligns with the knowledge and perspective I want to share. If you're curious about exactly how I used AI as a tool in this process, you'll find those details in Table 2.

**Table 2: How AI was used in the development of this book**

| Use of AI | Details |
|---|---|
| **1. Conducting market and customer research.** | AI helped me identify this book's target audience, their interests, needs, and key challenges. By streamlining market research and pinpointing the most relevant aspects of AI, I could tailor the content effectively. Saving countless hours on this task allowed me to focus on what matters most—writing a high-quality, valuable book. |
| **2. Reviewing books and analyzing their reviews.** | AI analyzed competing books and their customer reviews, helping me differentiate this book and enhance its value. By summarizing insights from hundreds of reviews, AI enabled me to shape the content to better meet your needs. |
| **3. Developing the book's structure and outline.** | Based on market research and book reviews, AI generated an outline and structure to ensure a natural flow and comprehensive coverage of key topics. While I guided the process, AI provided a valuable head start, allowing me to focus on writing, editing, and publishing more efficiently. |
| **4. Brainstorming ideas and trends.** | I used AI to brainstorm ideas and identify trends. While my guidance shaped the direction, AI processed information far faster than I could, saving time and providing valuable insights. |
| **5. Creating and editing interior images.** | I created most of the interior images in this book using AI-powered image generators. For those I didn't create, I used AI tools to edit and enhance them, showcasing the technology's potential. While a human designer crafted the book cover, AI generated its main image—a woman being created by AI. |
| **6. Editing and checking for plagiarism.** | AI tools like Grammarly and Quillbot provided cost-effective, time-efficient editing support. While I've worked with excellent human editors before, AI streamlined the process, allowing me to publish this book faster. These tools also helped check for potential plagiarism. |

Given AI's role in developing this book, is it still right for me to call myself the author? Absolutely, without question! I share this with you as the first example of generative AI in action included in this book to highlight the power and potential of this technology—not to replace humans but to enhance what we can achieve together.

Before we embark on this journey, I want to leave you with an empowering thought: No matter where you are in your AI journey, you have the potential to grow, adapt, and innovate. Generative AI rewards curiosity and exploration, so dive in, discover, and let the possibilities unfold.

# ONE
# FOUNDATIONS OF GENERATIVE AI

Have you ever:

- hummed a tune and wished you could turn it into a song or symphony?
- needed a personalized workout plan but did not want—or could not afford—to hire a trainer?
- struggled with a blank page, yearning for inspiration to strike?
- dreamed of creating your own comic or coloring book, but lacked the artistic skills?
- wanted to write a poem, a heartfelt message, or a message of condolence but couldn't find the right words?

These are just a few of the nearly endless ways in which generative AI can assist, inspire, and amplify human creativity.

# GENERATIVE ARTIFICIAL INTELLIGENCE EXPLAINED

Generative AI is a type of artificial intelligence that can create new content—such as human-like conversations, images, videos, 3D models, and music—based on data it has been trained on. This technology is akin to having a collaborator who never sleeps, generating fresh ideas and content upon demand.

## Neural Networks

At the root of generative AI lies deep learning, an advanced form of machine learning that involves multiple layers of artificial neurons. Each layer builds on knowledge gained from previous layers, helping AI recognize patterns, make predictions, and generate creative outputs.

"Glowing neural network." AI-generated using Midjourney.

*Artificial neural networks (ANNs)* form the backbone of deep learning, mimicking how the human brain processes information. These networks consist of layers of interconnected nodes (neurons) that work together to detect patterns and make predictions. Different types of neural networks serve different purposes. For example, *feed-forward neural networks (FNNs)* are the simplest type. They move information in one direction from input to output and are commonly used in basic AI models. *Recurrent neural networks (RNNs)* are designed for sequential data like speech and text. RNNs can remember previous inputs, making them useful for translation and speech recognition tasks. Next, *convolutional neural networks (CNNs)* are primarily used for image generation and processing. CNNs detect edges, textures, and patterns, making them fundamental in computer vision and AI-generated artwork. Finally, *transformer models* represent a significant advancement in AI architecture, enabling systems like ChatGPT and Claude to process and generate text with exceptional fluency. Unlike RNNs, which analyze text sequentially, transformers use a mechanism called self-attention to evaluate entire sentences simultaneously. This approach helps them retain context over longer passages, improving coherence and accuracy in text generation and understanding.

Generative AI models need to be trained, which is a complex process of teaching them how to learn by exposing them to vast data sets. During training, these models adjust their internal parameters to fine-tune their outputs. Essentially, they improve over time. This training is crucial, and the more diverse and richer the data sets, the better the model will perform.

This technology stands out for its adaptability and capacity to cater to different applications. Beyond content creation, generative AI also plays a vital role in data augmentation, which refers to artificially creating new data points—often by incrementally modifying existing data—to expand and diversify a dataset used to train machine learning models. It is about increasing the variety of data available for training and improving the model's performance by exposing it to more and more scenarios.

## Generative Versus Discriminative Models

Not all AI models generate new content. *Discriminative models* identify patterns in data to classify or predict an outcome. For example, an email spam filter discriminates between spam and non-spam emails. *Generative models*, on the other hand, create new data based on learned patterns. A generative model could produce a brand-new email that resembles a human-written message or generate realistic images of people who do not exist. There are many types of generative AI models. While all such models can produce new content, how they achieve this differs. For example, *variational autoencoders (VAEs)* generate images and music. They learn efficient data representations and generate variations similar to but distinct from the original data. *Generative adversarial networks (GANs)* are a widely used approach where two neural networks—the generator (which creates images, text, or video) and the discriminator (which tries to detect whether the output is real or AI-generated)—compete to improve output quality. GANs are behind hyper-realistic AI art and deepfake technology. *Diffusion Models* are used in high-quality image generation. They start with a completely messy, grainy picture—like static on a TV—and gradually refine it, step by step, until a clear, realistic image appears. This technology is changing how AI creates visuals, making it a powerful tool for photography, art, and design.

### Generative AI Architectures

Generative AI is not limited to text generation. Different AI architectures specialize in generating different types of content. For example, *generative pre-trained transformers (GPT)* are a model architecture that generates human-like text, powering applications like ChatGPT, Claude, and Jasper. *Bidirectional encoder representations from transformers (BERT)* are designed to understand text and are, therefore, widely used in search engines, sentiment analysis, and classification, with implementations such as Google Search. *Latent diffusion models (LDMs)* are the underlying architecture behind AI-generated image tools like DALL-E, Midjourney, and Stable Diffusion, which create visuals from text descriptions (or prompts). Finally, the *text-to-text transfer transformer (T5)* is designed to convert one text format into another. It is widely used in applications like Google Translate and AI-powered summarization tools.

## AI CLASSIFICATION FRAMEWORKS

To better understand artificial intelligence and generative AI's place within it, we can classify AI using two key frameworks: *what AI can do* and *what AI is used for*. Since generative AI often works alongside other AI types, exploring these distinctions is useful.

The first framework categorizes AI by capabilities—what it can do. *Reactive AI* has no memory and responds only to immediate stimuli. IBM's Deep Blue, which defeated chess champion Garry Kasparov in 1997, is a classic example. *Limited-memory AI* learns from past data to improve responses, which is how most modern AI, including deep learning models, function today. *Theory of mind AI*, still theoretical, would understand emotions, beliefs, and mental states, enhancing human-AI interaction. The most advanced stage, *self-aware AI*, theoretically possesses self-consciousness and independent thinking, making autonomous decisions beyond its programming.

The second framework classifies AI by purpose—what it is used for. *Narrow, or weak AI*, specializes in specific tasks, like language translation or image recognition. *General AI (AGI)*, which does not yet exist, would perform at human intelligence levels across multiple domains. *Artificial superintelligence, or super AI*, remains a theoretical concept, surpassing human intelligence entirely.

So, where does generative AI fit? It belongs to narrow AI, as it generates text, images, audio, and video within defined parameters. While tools like ChatGPT and DALL-E may seem far from "weak" given their sophistication, they still operate within predefined constraints rather than generalizing across domains like a human mind.

## TRADITIONAL, MODERN, AND GENERATIVE AI

The terms traditional AI and generative AI—a type of modern AI—are used extensively throughout this book. To understand their differences, think of traditional AI as a rule-follower, modern AI as a student who learns and improves over time, and generative AI as an artist who creates entirely new content.

“Traditional, modern, and generative AI depicted as women.” AI-generated using DALL-E.

These distinctions matter because AI systems often work together to achieve results. Many real-world examples in this book highlight how different types of AI interact, helping you see their practical applications in everyday life and work.

To further examine the nuances of traditional, modern, and generative AI, I invite you to review Table 3.

**Table 3: Differences between traditional, modern, and generative AI**

| Feature | Traditional AI | Modern AI | Generative AI |
|---|---|---|---|
| **Core Function** | Rule-following | Learning and predicting | Creating new content |
| **Flexibility and Adaptability** | Limited to pre-programmed rules | Learns and adapts from data | Generates unique, creative outputs across many domains |
| **Example Tasks** | Email spam filtering | Fraud detection in banking | Image generation |
| | Calculating loan eligibility based on fixed criteria | Predicting real estate prices and stock market trends | Writing content |
| | Basic robotics in manufacturing; robots performing repetitive tasks | Image recognition in social media | Composing music |
| **Human Interaction (How the AI interacts with or supports humans)** | Minimal, predefined, task-specific | Dynamic, conversational | Creative, personal |
| | Humans provide specific inputs and the AI outputs results based on fixed rules. | Processes human inputs like speech, text, or images and adapts responses to the user, improving over time. | Takes human inputs and generates new, custom outputs, mimicking creative or conversational human behavior. |

Despite its promise, generative AI is often misunderstood. For example, some believe it will fully replace human creativity, but that's a misconception. While AI can generate surprisingly intricate content, it does so by analyzing vast amounts of existing data, identifying patterns, and recombining elements in new ways. In essence, it creates 'new' content by drawing from what already exists—it doesn't think, feel, or create in the way humans do.

This is why AI-generated work, no matter how sophisticated, lacks the emotional depth, lived experience, and intuition human creators bring. It is a tool—a powerful one—but still a tool that I believe is best used to complement human effort rather than replace it. When applied thoughtfully, generative AI can enhance creativity by expanding possibilities, automating tedious tasks, and providing inspiration, but the final touch—true originality—remains uniquely human.

Researchers evaluate AI-generated outputs using established metrics to ensure they meet quality and reliability standards. For example, *perplexity* (not to be confused with the AI search engine bearing the same name) measures how well an AI predicts the next word in a sequence. *BLEU (Bilingual Evaluation Understudy)* scores assess the accuracy of AI-generated translations. And for AI-generated images, the *Fréchet Inception Distance (FID)* metric is used. This metric compares generated images to real ones to determine their realism and coherence.

These evaluation techniques help refine models, improve accuracy, and enhance the overall quality of AI-generated content.

Another issue is the abuse of AI. Nefarious actors can, do, and will continue to intentionally misuse AI to spread disinformation—false information deliberately created and spread to deceive, manipulate, or mislead people—often for political, financial, or ideological purposes.

Like any technology, AI requires ethical guidelines and responsible usage. Understanding these limitations helps us appreciate the true potential of generative AI without overestimating its capabilities. In Chapter 8, we will explore these and other ethical issues and limitations in greater detail.

The significance of generative AI in today's technological landscape cannot be overstated. It represents a shift towards innovation-driven processes in creative industries, allowing for automated content generation that maintains quality and creativity. This shift is particularly impactful in sectors like media, where AI assists in tasks such as color correction and sound editing, which enhances production quality and efficiency.

AI will undoubtedly continue developing and evolving. As it does, its role in transforming industries becomes increasingly apparent, as it offers new opportunities for innovation and growth and pushes the boundaries of what's possible in this digital era.

## LARGE LANGUAGE MODELS

### Unpacking the Basics

Large language models, or LLMs, are the powerhouse behind many of today's AI-driven text applications. They rely on deep learning and intricate neural networks that mimic certain aspects of human cognition, particularly pattern recognition. As we learned earlier, these models consist of multiple layers of interconnected nodes, each processing and refining information before passing it to the next.

For example, the initial layers of a neural network might detect basic linguistic features such as individual words or characters, while deeper layers analyze more complex structures like grammar, sentence composition, and contextual meaning. This hierarchical processing enables LLMs to understand and generate human-like text by capturing nuances in language.

The architecture includes millions—sometimes billions—of parameters, which help fine-tune the model's ability to produce coherent, grammatically correct, and contextually relevant output. This immense scale and complexity make LLMs invaluable for a wide range of applications, such as summarization and research assistance, language translation, diagnostics support, creative writing, chatbots, policy drafting, interview and resume assistance, and much more.

Training these massive LLMs requires enormous amounts of data and substantial computational power. The process starts with data collection, where developers compile text from diverse sources such as books, articles, and websites. Some have even described generative AI as 'absorbing the entirety of the internet,' highlighting its extensive reliance on publicly available information.

This data, which can amount to terabytes* of information for large-scale AI models, undergoes preprocessing to keep it clean and relevant. Preprocessing steps may include removing duplicates, handling missing values, and normalizing formats. Once prepared, the data is fed into the model for training—a phase requiring high-performance computing resources. Complex calculations are handled by specialized hardware, such as Graphics Processing Units (GPUs) and Tensor Processing Units (TPUs), which accelerate the process with their parallel processing capabilities.

Training can take weeks or months, depending on the model's size and complexity. The model aims to learn patterns and relationships within the data, enabling it to generate accurate and meaningful text. However, this process isn't just about raw power; it also requires careful tuning and evaluation to verify the model's performance meets the desired standards.

LLMs find applications across various sectors, transforming how businesses operate and interact with customers. In customer service, companies deploy chatbots powered by LLMs to handle inquiries and complaints. These chatbots can understand and respond to many questions, providing consistent support around the clock. In content creation, LLMs assist writers by generating article drafts, editing text, and even suggesting headlines, which speeds up production and can help writers deliver higher-quality work faster. Beyond customer service and content creation, LLMs are making waves in fields like education, where they help develop personalized learning materials, and in healthcare, where they support diagnostic tools by processing and analyzing vast amounts of medical literature.

Despite their impressive capabilities, LLMs have notable limitations. One major challenge is potential bias in training data, where

* To put a terabyte into perspective, a scanned text page is roughly 0.01 MB in size. One terabyte could store about one million pages—equivalent to the paper produced from approximately 50,000 trees. This immense storage capacity is enough to comfortably archive a lifetime of personal memories or the digital content of many small businesses!

the model can learn and reproduce societal prejudices. Addressing this issue requires careful curation, ongoing evaluation, and proactive bias mitigation strategies. Another concern is data privacy, as the large datasets used for training could include sensitive information. Ensuring robust privacy measures is essential to protecting user data and maintaining security.

The scale of LLMs also raises concerns about energy consumption. Researchers are addressing this challenge by optimizing training processes, such as focusing only on essential data, simplifying mathematical operations, and using smaller, higher-quality datasets. Fine-tuning existing models for specific tasks, rather than building them from scratch, has helped reduce energy and resource use as well. Custom hardware like Google's TPUs and NVIDIA's GPUs improve processing efficiency, while innovations in server cooling systems further reduce environmental impacts. Additionally, adaptive models that adjust computing power based on task complexity are being developed along with smaller, task-specific models to minimize energy use. Many companies are also transitioning to renewable energy sources to power their AI systems, further contributing to the effort to reduce the energy footprint of LLMs.

## Core Concepts

This section introduces you to the core concepts of LLMs. Understanding how LLMs work will give you a deeper appreciation of this technology, which I think is vital for all users of generative AI to understand.

### *Tokenization*

LLMs have a fascinating way of understanding and processing text, making them incredibly powerful. At the heart of this process is something called tokenization. Tokenization is like breaking a long sentence into bite-sized pieces, each representing a token. These tokens could be whole words, parts of words, or even individual characters. By deconstructing language into smaller, manageable chunks, LLMs can better analyze and understand the text. This method allows the models to grasp the nuances of language to help them generate coherent and meaningful responses.

### *Embeddings*

Embeddings also play a crucial role in how LLMs work. Think of embeddings as compact digital representations of words, where each word is assigned a unique set of numbers that capture its meaning and how it relates to other words. These numerical representations help the model figure out context and intent, like mapping social network relationships. LLMs can use both embeddings and tokenization to deliver contextually relevant and insightful responses.

### *Transformer Architecture*

As you may recall from our earlier discussion about neural networks, transformer models represent a revolutionary building block of modern LLMs, transforming how these models process language. At its core is the self-attention mechanism, which enables the model to consider all parts of a sentence simultaneously rather than analyzing it word by word. This concept can be conceived as having a highlighter that simultaneously marks multiple key phrases in a document, ensuring the most relevant parts are connected and understood in context. Self-attention lets the model determine which words are most important in relation to others, helping it grasp the deeper meaning of a sentence. This approach mimics how humans might glance back at earlier parts of a sentence to understand its whole meaning, but it does so with incredible speed and precision. By processing information in parallel instead of sequentially, transformers work faster and produce more accurate and contextually aware text. This innovation has made transformers the foundation of today's most advanced language models, powering tools that handle everything from creative writing to complex technical tasks with remarkable sophistication.

### *Transfer Learning*

Another key concept is transfer learning. This involves taking a pre-trained model, which already understands language to some extent, and fine-tuning it for specific tasks. This process is akin to hiring a generalist who can quickly adapt to specialized roles. Instead of starting from scratch, transfer learning allows models to utilize existing knowledge, saving time and resources. For instance, a model trained on vast amounts of general text can be fine-tuned for legal document analysis, making it adept at understanding legal jargon and nuances. This adaptability makes transfer learning a powerful tool, enabling LLMs to be applied across diverse domains with remarkable efficiency and effectiveness.

### *Model Scaling*

Model scaling is another fascinating aspect of LLMs. As models grow with more parameters and larger datasets, they often perform better, capturing subtleties in language that smaller models might miss. However, this improvement comes with trade-offs. More extensive models require more computational power and resources, making them costly to deploy and maintain. It is like upgrading from a compact car to a luxury SUV. While gaining power and features, you also face higher expenses, like maintenance and gas consumption. Despite these challenges, the benefits of increased accuracy and performance often justify the investment, especially in fields that demand precision and detail.

### Key Takeaway

Understanding these core concepts of tokenization, embeddings, transformers, transfer learning, and model scaling provides a solid foundation for appreciating the complexities and capabilities of LLMs. They are the building blocks that enable these models to perform a wide range of tasks, from natural language processing (NLP) to sophisticated content generation. As AI continues to evolve, these elements will remain crucial in shaping how we interact with and benefit from this technology. The potential applications are vast, and the journey to fully realizing them is just beginning; the impact of LLMs will be profound, changing industries and enhancing our interactions with technology in ways we are only beginning to fully appreciate.

* * *

## CHAPTER 1 SELF-ASSESSMENT

Ready to test your understanding of this chapter and reinforce your learning? Scan the QR code below or enter the following URL into your browser to take the short quiz! URL: [**https://tinyurl.com/GenAI-Ch1-Quiz**].

QR code to access the Chapter 1 quiz.

## TWO
# TOOLS OF THE TRADE

From conversational chatbots to image generators and AI-powered audio tools, these technologies are transforming industries and redefining creativity. In this chapter, we will explore a range of cutting-edge generative AI tools, their unique applications, and the opportunities they offer. We will also discuss the challenges of their use and how they're shaping the future of work, art, and technology. Kai-Fu Lee, a pioneer in artificial intelligence and a leading tech investor, captured this vision perfectly at the 2018 EmTech Digital conference when he said:

> *The real promise of AI is not automation — it's augmentation, helping humans to think and create in ways we've never imagined.*

Lee's perspective underscores how generative AI is not about replacing human effort; rather, it is about amplifying our capabilities, sparking innovation, and unlocking new forms of expression in virtually every field.

## THE AI TOOLBOX

AI tools come in many forms and serve a wide range of purposes across industries. While there are multiple ways to categorize them, a useful distinction is between tools built entirely around AI and those that integrate AI into existing functionalities. For simplicity, we can group them into two broad categories: *generative AI tools* and *AI-enhanced tools*. The former are designed primarily to create new content using AI, whether text, images, video, or audio. Examples include ChatGPT, Claude, Jasper, DALL-E, and Synthesia. The latter are existing platforms incorporating AI to improve their core functions, such as writing, design, automation, or analytics. Examples include Microsoft Copilot, Google Gemini, Grammarly, Canva, and Zapier.* Of course, these are not the only ways to categorize AI tools as many tools also blur the lines between these groups, but this categorization does provide a practical, easy-to-remember framework for our discussion.

With so many AI tools available, it's easy to feel overwhelmed by the sheer number of options. Rather than scrambling to keep up with every new tool—an approach some online courses promote—I recommend starting with a specific problem you need to solve or a task you want to improve. From there, you can identify the right AI tool (or combination of tools) to meet your needs. The following example illustrates this approach to choosing the right AI tools to solve a specific problem.

**Example: Repurposing webinar content**

*Problem:* A 2-person marketing team at a mid-sized nonprofit organization hosts a 60-minute educational webinar every month. After the event, they need to:

---

* Entire chapters—or even a whole book—could be dedicated to exploring the vast array of AI tools, but that's not the focus here. While I will discuss some tools in more detail, I encourage you to conduct supplementary research if you would like to learn more about these or other AI tools.

- *Transcribe the webinar* for reference and accessibility.
- *Summarize key takeaways* for a blog post.
- *Extract short clips* for social media.
- *Create an email follow-up* with highlights for attendees.
- *Improve SEO (search engine optimization)* performance for blog content.

This process is time-consuming and requires multiple manual steps. The team needs an efficient way to automate these tasks while maintaining quality.

*Solution:* After discussing their problem, the team selects a combination of tools for efficiency. The tools they choose include:

- *Otter.ai* → Automated transcription. Otter.ai converts the webinar audio into text, making extracting quotes and key points quicker and easier.
- *Claude (pro version)* → Summarization and content drafting. Claude summarizes the key discussion points into a concise yet impactful blog post. It also helps the team generate an attendee follow-up email with key insights.
- *Descript* → Video editing and clip extraction. Descript allows the team to automatically identify highlights and create short clips for social media.
- *Semrush* → Optimizes content for SEO. Semrush helps the team optimize blog content by suggesting keywords and readability improvements to enhance search engine rankings.

*Outcome:* By leveraging this AI-powered workflow, the team saves hours of manual work while ensuring their content is high-quality, repurposable, and optimized for multiple platforms.

AI is already woven into our daily workflows, and understanding its capabilities allows us to use it more effectively and strategically rather than reactively. By knowing how these tools work, we can capitalize on their strengths while maintaining control over messaging, accuracy, and decision-making.

## CHATTING WITH AI

ChatGPT is a versatile conversational AI, capable of generating human-like responses across various topics and tones. It adapts seamlessly to different formats, as demonstrated in this interaction:

> **Me:** Write a haiku about the future of AI.
> **ChatGPT:** Machines learn and grow, / Whispers of code shape the world, / Tomorrow unfolds.
> **Me:** I like it! What if I wanted this in the style of Shakespeare?
> **ChatGPT:** O wondrous mind, where knowledge doth abound, / Through circuits vast, the future's threads are wound. / From mortal hands to engines vast and bright, / The dawn of thought breaks forth as boundless light.
> **Me:** Impressive! Now, please make it a sci-fi movie tagline.
> **ChatGPT:** *In a world where machines dream… the future awakens.*

This exchange highlights ChatGPT's ability to shift creative styles instantly—from poetry to Shakespearean prose to punchy marketing copy.

Beyond content creation, ChatGPT is transforming industries. Many businesses integrate it into websites and apps via APIs to automate customer support, handle FAQs, and resolve common issues, freeing up human agents for complex inquiries. It also enhances user interactions and provides insights into customer behavior. Companies can fine-tune response styles to align with brand messaging, ensuring consistency. In education, ChatGPT helps students grasp complex concepts, simulate real-world scenarios, and practice language skills. Marketers use it to generate engaging blog posts, social media content, and promotional materials tailored to different audiences.

Aaron Levie, co-founder and CEO of Box, compares ChatG-PT's impact to past technological breakthroughs like Google and the iPhone. On X (Dec 4, 2022), he noted:

> *There's a certain feeling that happens when a new technology adjusts your thinking about computing. Google did it. Firefox did it. AWS did it. iPhone did it. OpenAI is doing it with ChatGPT.*

This highlights ChatGPT as more than just a productivity tool—it's reshaping how we interact with technology. Just as past innovations altered our digital habits, ChatGPT has the potential to redefine AI's role in everyday work, unlocking more intuitive and creative ways of operating.

Other popular conversational AI tools include Microsoft Copilot, Perplexity.ai, Jasper, Google Gemini, and Claude, each with different strengths. Microsoft Copilot integrates into Word, Excel, and Teams for productivity, while Perplexity.ai functions as an AI-powered search engine. Jasper excels in marketing and content generation, Google Gemini enhances Google Search, and Claude prioritizes safety, context retention, and long-form reasoning.

Despite their strengths, conversational AI tools have limitations. They may misinterpret context, handle sensitive topics poorly, or produce hallucinations—confident yet false information. This is especially concerning in fields where accuracy is critical. AI has misinterpreted legal text, producing incorrect summaries, or confidently provided false answers to public inquiries.

Why do hallucinations happen? AI doesn't truly "understand" information—it predicts responses based on training data, which may contain both facts and inaccuracies. Many AI models don't access live data, relying on static training sets that sometimes combine information in misleading ways. The takeaway? AI can assist, but humans must verify.

Managing conversational context is another challenge, as AI can lose track of discussion flow. Clear guidelines and refined prompts help mitigate these risks, ensuring chatbots remain reliable and context aware. Techniques like prompt engineering and reinforcing context (explored in Chapter 4) can also improve coherence. Additionally, AI-generated responses can be fine-tuned through continuous adjustments, ensuring interactions remain high-quality, relevant, and trustworthy.

APIs play a crucial role in integrating AI tools into business workflows. They enable seamless communication between applications, automating tasks, improving productivity, and enhancing user experiences. For example, an e-commerce platform can process payments via Stripe's API without building a payment system from scratch—similarly, APIs allow AI chatbots to function within websites and apps without extensive customization.

## GENERATING CODE

For a moment, place yourself in a high-stakes coding competition where time is limited and the pressure is on to deliver high-quality code. In this situation, tools like AlphaCode and GitHub Copilot become invaluable. GitHub Copilot and other popular code generation tools such as Amazon Q Developer, Tabnine, and Replit utilize generative AI to transform how developers approach coding tasks.

Unlike traditional AI, which focuses on debugging and analyzing code, generative AI actively creates code solutions based on context. These tools do more than suggest lines of code—they generate intelligent, contextually relevant snippets that streamline development. GitHub Copilot, for example, suggests entire code structures as you type, reducing the need for repetitive boilerplate coding. This real-time assistance allows developers to focus on complex challenges, boosting efficiency and reducing stress.

Many of these tools integrate seamlessly into existing workflows. GitHub Copilot works within popular Integrated Development Environments (IDEs) like Visual Studio Code, supporting multiple programming languages such as Python and JavaScript. It predicts intent, suggesting next steps or even full functions based on context, enhancing productivity and coding precision.

While similar in function, AlphaCode is designed for competitive programming and excels at generating solutions for algorithmic challenges. It provides a foundation for tackling complex problems and often identifies novel approaches that would take significant time to conceptualize.

The impact of generative AI in coding is profound. Teams on tight deadlines can automate routine tasks like writing unit tests, implementing API integrations, or formatting code to meet style guidelines. By handling these repetitive tasks, AI allows developers to focus on logic and architecture, accelerating development while maintaining code quality.

However, AI-powered code generation comes with challenges. Over-reliance on AI can lead to blind spots, as AI-generated code isn't always flawless. Developers must stay engaged, critically assess outputs, and ensure they understand the logic behind AI-generated code. Errors, inefficiencies, or inconsistencies are possible, so rigorous review and testing are essential. Combining static code analysis tools with manual oversight helps verify correctness and optimize performance. With this balance of human expertise and AI assistance, developers can harness generative AI's full potential while maintaining high-quality, reliable code.

## EXPLORING VISUAL CREATIVITY

You've likely encountered AI-generated images from tools like DALL-E, Midjourney, Ideogram, and Stable Diffusion—or even created some yourself. If so, you know the thrill of describing a scene and watching it materialize in moments.

These AI tools act like digital artists, transforming text descriptions into stunning visual creations. They don't just generate pictures—they're reshaping how we approach art and design. By interpreting complex inputs, they produce everything from realistic portraits to surreal fantasy scenes, pushing creative boundaries for artists, designers, and creators alike.

What sets tools like DALL-E apart is their customization. Users can tweak prompts to achieve specific styles—whether a retro aesthetic or modern minimalism—ensuring they guide the AI's creativity rather than the other way around. These tools also enable artistic experimentation, making styles like expressionism, cubism, or Fauvism accessible, even for those without traditional artistic training.

To illustrate the flexibility of AI image generation tools, I asked DALL-E to create two images of Laika, the space dog. Laika was a small, mixed-breed dog, frequently described as part terrier or spitz. She lived as a stray on the streets of Moscow before becoming the first living being sent into orbit. She traveled to outer space inside Sputnik 2, which included life-support systems to provide oxygen and food and sensors to monitor her vital signs. She successfully orbited the earth, but sadly, she did not survive her space mission.

Laika is remembered as a trailblazer in space exploration, and her accomplishments are honored by a monument in Moscow.

"Laika the Space Dog: Two Ways." Left: Lifelike depiction of Laika. Right: Art Deco-style image of Laika. Both images were generated using DALL-E from text prompts.

With great power comes great responsibility. DALL-E and similar tools can generate strikingly realistic images, raising ethical concerns. One major issue is intellectual property rights—these tools must create without infringing on existing works or mimicking styles too closely. Another risk is misuse, such as producing deepfakes or misleading visuals that spread misinformation.

Many deepfake images have sparked controversy, including the viral 'Balenciaga Pope'—an AI-generated image of Pope Francis wearing a white puffer jacket styled like a luxury Balenciaga design. The image was so realistic that it fooled millions, highlighting the power and risks of AI-generated content. Chapter 8 will dive deeper into these and other ethical challenges in greater detail.

Author's renditions of "Balenciaga Pope." AI-generated using Midjourney.

## CREATING VIDEO WITH AI

Suppose you need to produce a captivating video under a tight deadline or simply want to experiment with AI's video creation capabilities. AI tools like Tencent's Cloud AI Digital Human Video Generator are transforming video production by generating realistic digital humans who can deliver scripts in multiple languages with natural expressions and gestures—at a fraction of the time and cost of traditional methods. Businesses can input text prompts, and the tool creates a lifelike presenter, revolutionizing advertising, education, and customer support.

Generative AI video tools, including Tencent's AI Video Generator, OpenAI's Sora, Runway's Gen-3 Alpha, Synthesia, and Pictory, offer significant advantages. Teams can automate tasks like creating spokesperson videos or localized ads, allowing creators to focus on strategy and storytelling. This accelerates workflows, especially for projects needing personalized, multilingual content. As I write this, a colleague is developing a self-paced online course on infrastructure and public-private partnerships for government officials worldwide using Synthesia. From what I've seen, it looks incredibly engaging—surprising, perhaps, given the subject matter.

AI-generated videos are becoming so realistic that many find the rapid progress unsettling. YouTube, TikTok, X, and Reddit are flooded with examples. In 2023, an AI-generated video of Will Smith eating spaghetti went viral. Grotesque and absurd, it seemingly sparked a trend of weird AI-generated videos. By 2024, AI-powered meme videos—including *The Distracted Boyfriend, Side-eyed Chloe, Trumpet Boy,* and *Zuckerberg is Watching*—began going viral, fueled by Luma Labs' Dream Machine. The meme names alone are hilarious, and if you haven't seen them, you might get a good laugh before realizing how eerily realistic AI videos are becoming. Soon—very soon—we may struggle to distinguish real from fake. We'll explore that more in Chapter 9.

## ENHANCING AUDIO AND VOICE APPLICATIONS

Suppose for a moment you're producing a podcast with voices indistinguishable from your favorite sports broadcasters. Or imagine yourself as an astute music enthusiast, listening to a classic song reimagined in another language.

A recent example is Universal Music Group's 2024 release of *"Noche Buena y Navidad,"* a Spanish rendition of Brenda Lee's 1958 hit *"Rockin' Around the Christmas Tree."* Using advanced AI, the original English vocals were seamlessly converted into Spanish, preserving Brenda Lee's voice while creating an entirely new cultural experience.

You can listen to it by visiting: **[https://tinyurl.com/Rockin Christmas-Spanish]**.

Generative AI audio tools offer customization, adaptability, and creative flexibility. Users can fine-tune voices for various applications, from soothing meditation apps to energetic educational tools. AI makes sound experimentation easier than ever, empowering creators to explore both realistic and fantastical soundscapes.

"Modern minimalist Christmas tree with swirling music notes." AI-generated using DALL-E.

However, these advancements come with challenges. Voice identity theft—where voices are cloned without consent—is a growing concern. The ability to replicate voices raises ethical and authenticity questions. Poor AI implementation can also produce unnatural-sounding audio, misaligned vocal inflections, or a lack of emotional depth, detracting from the user experience in podcasts or audiobooks. Establishing guidelines and transparency measures, including explicit consent for voice cloning, is crucial to ensuring ethical AI usage.

## SINGLE MODALITY VERSUS MULTIMODAL AI

Generative AI tools fall into two main categories: single modality AI and multimodal AI. The key distinction lies in how they process and generate content.

Single modality AI specializes in one type of content, such as text, images, audio, or video. These tools excel in their specific domain but require multiple AI systems when working across different media types. For example, a text-based AI like ChatGPT generates written content, while an image-generation model like DALL-E creates visuals—but they don't inherently interact with one another.

By contrast, multimodal AI can process and generate multiple types of content within the same system. These models integrate text, images, audio, and sometimes even video, allowing users to create more complex and cohesive outputs without switching between tools. For instance, a multimodal model like GPT-4 Vision can analyze an image and generate a written description in response, bridging different content types in a single workflow.

Most of the tools discussed so far are single modality AI tools. However, multimodal AI models offer a more integrated approach, streamlining workflows and enhancing efficiency by handling multiple data types simultaneously. To further illustrate the difference between the two, we will consider how single modality and multimodal AI can be used to develop a product marketing campaign.

### Approach 1: Developing a Marketing Campaign using Single Modality AI Tools

With single modality AI, different tools are used for each aspect of the campaign:

1. *ChatGPT* generates the product description and social media ad copy.
2. *DALL-E or Midjourney* creates high-quality promotional images.
3. *Runway ML* produces a short product video based on the AI-generated images.
4. *ElevenLabs* generates a realistic AI voiceover for the video.
5. *Whisper* transcribes and summarizes customer testimonials for blog and social media content.

This approach allows users to select the best AI tool for each task, ensuring high-quality results; however, switching between tools can be time-consuming, and maintaining consistency across different media formats requires additional effort.

### Approach 2: Developing a Marketing Campaign using Multimodal AI for a Seamless Workflow

With multimodal AI, a single model can handle most—if not all—of the tasks in one place:

1. The marketer inputs a request into Gemini 2.0 or GPT-4 Vision, asking for a product description, ad copy, and a high-quality product image in one step.
2. The same model also writes a video script based on the campaign theme.
3. Runway Gen-2 takes the AI-generated image and script and produces a 10-second promotional video with an AI-generated voiceover without requiring a separate narration tool.
4. If the marketer has a customer review video, GPT-4 Vision can transcribe, summarize, and extract the best highlights for social media posts.

### Choosing the Right Approach

Both single modality and multimodal AI have distinct advantages and limitations. The right approach depends on project complexity, cost considerations, and the need for specialized outputs. By understanding the tradeoffs with each approach, businesses and creators can determine which one best suit their needs. Table 4 on the following page highlights these systems' advantages and disadvantages.

**Table 4: Advantages and disadvantages of single modality and multimodal AI**

| Category | Single-modality AI | Multimodal AI |
|---|---|---|
| Advantages | • Highly specialized for specific tasks, often yielding superior results.<br>• Offers greater control and fine-tuning.<br>• Lower computational costs as individual AI models are more resource-efficient. | • Integrates multiple content types in a single system, reducing tool-switching and saving time.<br>• Ensures greater consistency across media formats.<br>• Ideal for tasks requiring seamless blending of different media types. |
| Disadvantages | • Requires switching between multiple tools, increasing manual effort and project time.<br>• Potential for inconsistencies in style and tone when combining outputs from different AI tools. | • Higher computational resource demands, increasing costs.<br>• Broad functionality can sometimes compromise quality for specific tasks. |

## Looking Ahead

As multimodal AI continues to evolve, its capabilities and limitations will become even more relevant across industries. Later in the book, Chapters 7 and 13 will further explore its applications, emerging trends, and growing role in AI-driven innovation.

* * *

## CHAPTER 2 SELF-ASSESSMENT

Do you think you've fully grasped this chapter? See for yourself by taking the end-of-chapter quiz by scanning the QR code or entering the following URL into your browser: [**https://tinyurl.com/GenAI-Ch2-Quiz**].

QR code to access the Chapter 2 quiz.

# THREE
# TRADITIONAL AND GENERATIVE AI WORKING TOGETHER

While traditional AI focuses on analyzing patterns and providing reliable solutions, generative AI takes creativity and adaptability to new heights. In this chapter, we will explore how these two forms of AI complement each other. By understanding their combined potential, you'll discover how this powerful partnership can enhance productivity, promote creativity, and redefine what's possible across various domains.

## FROM IDEA TO ARTICLE IN MINUTES

Generative AI can turn a spark of an idea into a fully fleshed-out, edited, and properly sourced article in minutes. AI-powered writing tools enhance productivity and creativity and help writers overcome the dreaded writer's block—that moment of staring at a blank screen, struggling to find the perfect opening line. Previously daunting tasks like writing articles, novels, blogs, or social media posts can become enjoyable and efficient with AI.

I can attest to this from personal experience. When I started my company, Clover Lane Publishing, I realized I needed help with tasks generative AI could support, such as designing the company's website, drafting content, and brainstorming blog and social media ideas. Having never built a website from scratch, I found the task daunting, especially alongside writing and publishing books. By outsourcing parts of these tasks to AI, I built a website in hours instead of days and generated over 50 unique ideas for blog and social media posts. Beyond saving time, the process was incredibly rewarding. I gained valuable skills, like understanding website design, and the content generated through AI brainstorming was varied, engaging, and occasionally delightfully unexpected. Without AI, I would have struggled to come up with so many compelling topics about publishing and the author's journey.

AI's capabilities extend beyond drafting and brainstorming. Tools like Grammarly and Quillbot were indispensable when editing this book. While these tools incorporate elements of generative AI, they primarily rely on traditional AI techniques, such as rule-based systems and machine learning algorithms, to enhance clarity, grammar, and originality. Traditional AI excels at processing structured data, applying predefined rules, and recognizing patterns, which makes these tools highly effective for tasks like error detection and stylistic consistency. They also serve as effective plagiarism checkers by identifying overlaps with existing works. These tools streamlined the often-meticulous revision process, ensuring the content remained polished and consistent throughout.

Generative AI also helps writers explore styles, from casual and friendly to authoritative or empathetic. For content requiring a specific voice or brand identity, AI can analyze previous work and adapt to match it, ensuring consistency across platforms. This adaptability is invaluable for businesses communicating with diverse audiences, allowing for tone adjustments tailored to cultural contexts or audience preferences. It also guarantees that messages resonate effectively, no matter the medium.

While AI's writing capabilities are impressive, challenges remain. One significant issue is maintaining originality in a world increasingly reliant on machine-generated content. Striking a balance between AI assistance and human creativity is crucial to preserving the final product's unique perspective. AI should enhance, not replace, the creative process. This requires human oversight to critically evaluate and refine AI-generated content, adding personal insights only humans can provide.

There is also the risk of overreliance on AI, which can stifle creativity if not managed carefully. AI is a powerful tool, but its full potential is realized only when combined with human ingenuity. By leveraging AI thoughtfully, you can maximize its benefits while preserving the authenticity and creativity that make your writing uniquely yours.

## VISUAL MEDIA TRANSFORMED

In digital art, generative AI acts as a new medium. It offers artists possibilities that were once unimaginable. Artists can now collaborate with generative AI tools to produce unique paintings or illustrations in specific styles that might otherwise take years to become proficient in. For instance, tools like DALL-E or Midjourney allow users to input prompts and instantly receive creative outputs ranging from abstract designs to hyper-realistic renderings. Recall the two images of Laika, the space dog, in Chapter 2. Laika took on two looks—one lifelike, the other art-deco. These tools enable artists to experiment with forms, colors, styles, and textures at the click of a button. What sets generative AI apart is its ability to generate thousands of iterations of a single idea, providing artists with many options to refine their visions. Traditional AI plays a complementary role here by analyzing user preferences or historical artistic trends to suggest which styles or iterations may resonate best. Together, generative and traditional AI streamline the creative process while balancing intuition and automation. Beyond generating individual pieces, generative AI is also a driving force behind augmented reality installations. In these immersive spaces, art evolves dynamically based on audience interaction. A gallery may, for example, feature digital murals that change shape and color as visitors move closer or linger, creating a personalized experience that transforms traditional notions of static art.

Generative AI is also revolutionizing pre- and post-production processes in film and animation. Storyboarding, typically a labor-intensive step, can now be enhanced and streamlined using generative AI, which creates visual concepts based on script inputs. Thanks to AI, directors can visualize scenes from multiple angles or experiment with lighting configurations before filming. This integration blends traditional AI for scene analysis and pattern recognition with generative AI's ability to craft detailed, adaptive visuals.

In post-production, AI-generated special effects set new standards for seamless computer-generated imagery (CGI) integration. By creating lifelike textures, weather effects, or even entire characters, generative AI reduces production time and costs. For example, software like Runway ML can create realistic environments or transform raw footage into polished cinematic sequences. With the support of traditional AI, spotting and correcting inconsistencies in effects or optimizing rendering workflows is now a reality.

Photography has also entered a new era. Editing tasks, such as color correction, blemish removal, or background alterations, are now faster and more accessible to the masses than ever before. Tools like Photoshop's generative fill feature allow photographers to reimagine their work, seamlessly adding or removing elements from images. While traditional AI has long-powered features like automated tagging and categorization, generative AI takes it further by enabling creative transformations. A simple portrait, for instance, can be turned into a digital oil painting or a surreal composite image with minimal input. Such capabilities empower photographers to push their artistic boundaries without compromising quality.

As AI deeply integrates into creative processes, critical questions about authorship and authenticity emerge. Generative AI challenges traditional notions of creativity by acting as an autonomous creator. If a generative AI produces a painting or a film scene based on a prompt, who holds ownership—the artist who guided the AI, the programmer who developed the model, both, or neither? These dilemmas demand the development of clear guidelines and policies. Traditional AI often plays a supporting role here by identifying similarities between AI-generated works and existing copyrighted materials, helping to assess intellectual property risks. For example, if a generative AI tool inadvertently produces artwork resembling a well-known painting, traditional AI systems can flag it for review. Establishing frameworks for fair use and licensing is essential to preserving the integrity of creative industries and nurturing collaboration between humans and machines. We will come back to this topic later in this book.

Generative AI is blurring the boundaries between tradition and technology. While this technology unlocks extraordinary possibilities for innovation, its coexistence with traditional AI helps keep creativity efficient and expansive. This ongoing dialogue between human ingenuity and technological advancement invites us to rethink the meaning of art in the digital age, emphasizing the importance of balance, ethics, and the enduring spirit of creativity.

## INNOVATION IN BUSINESS REDEFINED

In today's dynamic marketplace, businesses harness AI to redefine marketing strategies, enhance operational efficiency, and improve decision-making processes. Generative AI, as we're learning, is uniquely capable of creating new and innovative outputs like personalized content and adaptive solutions. However, it often relies on or involves traditional AI systems, such as predictive analytics and data monitoring. Understanding where generative and traditional AI intersect helps businesses maximize their potential while appreciating their distinct contributions.

Generative AI has transformed how businesses approach marketing by enabling the creation of innovative, audience-specific content at scale. Where traditional AI identifies patterns in consumer data to recommend marketing strategies, generative AI directly produces creative assets based on such recommendations, such as personalized ad copy, promotional images, and dynamic videos. Never before have marketers been able to craft hundreds of ad variations in mere minutes, each tailored to specific audience segments, but they can now. Today, a marketing team might pair this ability with traditional AI systems to analyze consumer behavior, which can significantly influence the best time to launch a campaign or identify which products are trending within a demographic. To zero in on how traditional and generative AI work together, traditional AI pinpoints the "what" and "when," and generative AI delivers the "how."

This ensuing use case might be less obvious than others but is equally transformative. Generative AI is reimagining operational challenges like inventory management by creating dynamic models that simulate and adapt to different market conditions. Traditional AI typically focuses on monitoring stock levels, tracking demand trends, and adjusting supply chain parameters in real-time. Generative AI, however, adds a layer of creativity by generating "what-if" scenarios and suggesting adaptive solutions. For instance, a retailer preparing for a major shopping season could use generative AI to simulate various outcomes, such as fluctuating consumer demand or supplier delays. These simulations enable businesses to visualize potential scenarios and proactively optimize their inventory strategies, reducing risk and improving efficiency.

Generative and traditional AI collaborate effectively in customer service. Traditional AI powers chatbots and automated assistants to handle routine questions, while generative AI crafts nuanced, human-like responses for more complex interactions. For instance, a generative AI-powered virtual assistant could simulate empathy when responding to a customer complaint, suggest tailored solutions, and draft detailed follow-up emails. In a travel company scenario, traditional AI might identify a canceled flight while generative AI drafts a personalized email offering alternative itineraries and hotel recommendations. Together, they enhance customer satisfaction and reduce the workload on human agents.

In strategic decision-making, generative AI complements traditional AI by enhancing executives' interpretation of data and exploration of opportunities. Traditional AI processes vast datasets, identifies trends, and highlights risks, while generative AI generates adaptive reports, visual dashboards, and actionable insights. For example, traditional AI might calculate sales projections and competitor performance when analyzing market expansion. At the same time, generative AI creates a comprehensive report, including plausible scenarios such as shifts in consumer sentiment. This collaboration provides a more holistic view of strategic options, empowering executives to make informed decisions.

By acknowledging and understanding the roles of generative and traditional AI and how they work together, businesses can capitalize on both to reach their fullest potential.

## EMPOWERED ENTREPRENEURS

Creativity and innovation extend beyond the arts into every domain, from business to engineering. Generative AI catalyzes creativity by offering fresh perspectives, generating unconventional solutions, and automating tedious tasks, while traditional AI ensures data-driven precision and analytical support. This combination allows entrepreneurs to think outside the box while making informed decisions—a critical advantage in today's fast-paced, competitive markets.

For example, generative AI can instantly generate unique product ideas, compelling branding concepts, or out-of-the-box marketing campaigns during a brainstorming session, sparking ideas that might not emerge in a traditional setting. Meanwhile, traditional AI analyzes market trends, assesses feasibility, and predicts customer demand, ensuring that these creative concepts are backed by data.

Entrepreneurs across industries are already leveraging this synergy in many ways, including these:

- *Startups* use generative AI for rapid prototyping, generating multiple product variations before investing in manufacturing.
- *E-commerce businesses* optimize product descriptions and advertisements using AI-generated content while refining their pricing strategies with predictive analytics.
- *Tech founders* rely on AI to generate initial business plans, conduct competitor analysis, and even fine-tune investor pitch decks.

This fusion of AI-powered creativity and data-driven intelligence democratizes entrepreneurship, allowing solo founders and small businesses to compete with larger enterprises. However, while generative AI is a powerful brainstorming tool, it should be balanced with human intuition, industry expertise, and real-world testing. Entrepreneurs who learn to leverage AI as an assistant rather than a decision-maker can drive true innovation, making bold ideas actionable and scalable.

## PERSONAL DEVELOPMENT: EXPANDING SKILLS AND ENHANCING WELL-BEING

Have you ever wanted to learn a new language without the tedious grind of memorization and repetition? Generative AI is revolutionizing how we learn languages by building on traditional AI's adaptive algorithms to create a more interactive and engaging experience. Traditional AI analyzes your performance, adjusts difficulty levels, and personalizes lesson plans, while generative AI enhances learning by simulating real-life conversations, dynamically correcting pronunciation, and generating culturally relevant phrases.

For example, Duolingo and Rosetta Stone integrate both forms of AI to make language learning more immersive. Duolingo's role-playing exercises use generative AI to create interactive dialogues that mimic real-world conversations, allowing learners to practice speech in different contexts. Rosetta Stone's TruAccent speech recognition engine offers real-time pronunciation feedback, refining accents and helping learners build conversational confidence. This fusion of AI technologies accelerates learning while making the process more engaging. However, AI tools alone cannot replace human interaction—language nuances, idioms, and cultural fluency still require exposure to native speakers and real-world practice.

Beyond language learning, AI is reshaping how people learn to code. Traditional AI platforms assess user mistakes, track progress, and adapt exercises to match skill levels, while generative AI enhances coding education by generating custom coding problems, offering alternative solutions, and providing detailed explanations. AI-powered platforms like GitHub Copilot or ChatGPT can analyze learners' errors and suggest new ways to structure code, helping them see multiple solutions to the same problem. This approach bridges the gap between novice and expert, allowing structured guidance from traditional AI while fostering creativity and flexibility through generative AI.

However, there's a risk: Students who over rely on AI-generated solutions may struggle with independent problem-solving and debugging, weakening their ability to think critically as developers. To maximize AI's benefits, learners should treat these tools as enhancements rather than replacements for foundational programming skills.

Personal development isn't just about acquiring skills—it's also about well-being. AI-powered mental health tools are becoming increasingly sophisticated, with traditional AI handling mood tracking and behavioral analysis. At the same time, generative AI creates personalized therapeutic interactions, simulates empathetic conversations, and generates guided mindfulness exercises. Apps like Woebot and Wysa combine these AI approaches to offer real-time emotional support. Woebot, for instance, uses natural language processing to engage in chat-based therapy, providing cognitive behavioral therapy techniques tailored to users' concerns. Wysa generates personalized coping strategies, meditation scripts, and supportive dialogue that mimic human-like conversations.

While these AI-powered tools can offer immediate relief and accessibility, they should not replace professional mental health care. AI cannot fully grasp complex human emotions or provide the depth of understanding that a trained therapist can offer. Instead, these tools work best as supplementary aids, helping users build resilience, track their emotions, and access self-help techniques when human support isn't readily available.

Integrating generative AI into personal development can help individuals learn faster, gain new perspectives, and improve their well-being. However, striking the right balance—leveraging AI's strengths while maintaining critical thinking and human connection—is key to truly benefiting from these innovations.

* * *

## CHAPTER 3 SELF-ASSESSMENT

Let's see how much of this Chapter you've absorbed! Tackle the end-of-chapter quiz by scanning the QR code or entering this shortened link into your browser: [**https://tinyurl.com/GenAI-Ch3-Quiz**].

QR code to access the Chapter 3 quiz.

# FOUR
# PROMPT ENGINEERING ESSENTIALS

This chapter explores prompt engineering—the key to getting the best from AI. Think of AI as a skilled artist and your prompts as brushstrokes guiding its creation. A well-crafted prompt ensures precise, tailored responses, whether you're drafting proposals, composing music, or designing logos. The quality of your prompts directly shapes AI's output, determining whether it's spot-on, needs tweaking, or misses the mark.

This chapter is divided into two sections: one for beginners and another for those ready to explore advanced techniques. But whether you're new or experienced, reading the whole chapter can only help!

## PART 1: INTRODUCTION TO PROMPT ENGINEERING

## SHAPING AI OUTPUTS THROUGH PRECISION

Creating an effective prompt involves several key components, each contributing to the clarity and specificity of the interaction. To illustrate the importance of crafting an effective prompt, consider setting out on a journey without a map or even basic directions to the final destination—a sure recipe for confusion and failure to get where you need to be. Similarly, a prompt provided to an AI requires clear objectives and defined outcomes to guarantee it understands the task at hand. Providing contextual information and constraints is the equivalent of giving an AI a map and compass to help it navigate. A good prompt should be specific enough to guide the AI while leaving room for creativity, striking the right balance between instruction and inspiration to enable the AI to perform optimally.

Let us look at a potential example to illustrate this concept further. Consider asking AI to "write a story." What will the output be? We have no idea because the instructions are not specific. So, you could wind up with a fairy tale meant for a 12-year-old, a sci-fi thriller that might give you nightmares, or anything in between. Also, how long will the story be? A couple of pages or 100 or more? In truth, if you were to give a tool like ChatGPT an instruction to "write a story," it will not proceed until you give it further direction because that prompt is just too vague.

Consider revising your prompt to something more specific: "Write a story about a purple and blue female dragon named Alera who learns to fly a helicopter over the Grand Canyon." In this second example, the AI has much more information to go on; it better "understands" the kind of story you're looking for. You can take it a step further by including the desired length of the story (let's say 500-words), and the style of writing you want the AI to use (perhaps, in this case, humorous?). The more specific example will yield a much more focused and relevant response, likely meeting your vision or coming close to it. In short, specificity enhances the quality of the output and is more likely to align with your expectations.

Here is an excerpt of what I got from ChatGPT when I prompted it to write such a story:

*In a world where dragons and humans coexisted, Alera, a purple-and-blue-scaled dragon, was not your average fire-breather. While her peers roasted marshmallows with their fiery snorts or showed off their aerial barrel rolls, Alera had a peculiar dream—to fly a helicopter. Yes, a helicopter. "Why flap when you can rotor?" she often mused....*

Testing different prompts is an essential part of the process, and fortunately, several platforms allow users to experiment and refine their inputs. OpenAI's playground is popular as it offers a space to test prompt variations and observe how the AI responds. This interactive environment provides real-time feedback, enabling you to tweak and adjust prompts until you achieve the desired outcome. Other platforms, like PromptHub, Promptmetheus, and Reprompt, offer similar capabilities, allowing users to evaluate AI performance and improve prompt effectiveness. By engaging in this iterative process, you can refine your skills and develop a deeper understanding of how prompts influence AI behavior, ultimately enhancing the quality of your interactions.

## CRAFTING EFFECTIVE PROMPTS: TECHNIQUES AND STRATEGIES

Iterative prompt development, a process that thrives on trial and error to refine and perfect your prompts, can be likened to entering a room filled with potential, where every word you use influences how AI responds.

This process begins with providing a prompt and analyzing the AI's output. Each response acts as a mirror, reflecting your prompt's effectiveness. Were the results what you anticipated? Did the AI grasp the nuances of your request? By scrutinizing these outputs, you can identify areas for improvement and adjust your language accordingly. This is where modifying your language for clarity becomes crucial. Consider each word an essential puzzle piece; altering one can transform the response. Through this iterative approach, you refine your prompts, aligning them more closely with your desired outcomes, ensuring that the AI understands and delivers precisely what you need.

As we learned, specificity is another vital element in crafting effective prompts. If you order a fruit salad, you will likely get cut-up fruit in a bowl, but you could also get fruit and lettuce mixed on a plate. Which output is the one you want? To get what you have in mind, you need to be specific. For example, you could ask for an evenly layered parfait with strawberries, blueberries, and a dollop of yogurt on the side. The more specific your prompt, the more tailored the AI's response will be. Using specific keywords and phrases helps reduce ambiguity, guiding the AI to focus on the task at hand. Defining constraints and parameters further sharpens this focus, setting boundaries within which the AI operates. This precision transforms a broad request into a targeted query, leading to improved relevance and utility of the AI's output.

Providing context and examples can also greatly enhance the quality of AI responses. Context is like establishing the setting of a story (will the story take place on a farm, in an urban environment, in the woods, in space, or somewhere else?). By embedding relevant details in your prompt, you offer the AI a comprehensive framework to draw upon, which improves its ability to generate outputs aligned with your vision. Providing illustrative examples is another form of guidance; examples help demonstrate what you're looking for from the AI. So, whether you are drafting a legal document for a business start-up or crafting a story in outer space, context and examples bridge the gap between intent and execution, leading to relevant and insightful responses.

Of course, even the best-laid plans can go awry, and prompt crafting is no exception. Common pitfalls often arise, but with awareness, they can be avoided. Overly complex prompts are one such trap, where the AI becomes bogged down by so many intricate instructions that they obscure the main objective. In this case, simplifying language and being concise are key deployment strategies.

## TEACHING THE ART AND SCIENCE OF PROMPT ENGINEERING

Many books and online resources on generative AI take the shortcut of providing readers with pre-made prompts for specific tasks. While this is convenient and likely appealing, this approach promotes dependence rather than empowerment. It's like the adage, "Give a person a fish, and they eat for a day. Teach a person to fish, and they eat for a lifetime." This book teaches you how to fish....well, how to engineer your prompts for AI outputs to be more accurate. I aim to teach you some methodologies to improve the effectiveness of prompt engineering so you will feel confident and capable of developing and adapting prompts to fit any scenario or task rather than relying on someone else's that may or may not be the right fit for your purpose. Self-reliance will serve you far better than memorizing a handful of static prompts.

### Method 1: Context, Clarity, and Refinement

The context, clarity, and refinement, or CCR methodology, is foundational in prompt engineering. It begins with establishing **context** by clearly defining the purpose of the prompt. Without context, the AI's response may be vague or irrelevant. For instance, asking "Explain AI" may result in a broad, unstructured answer. In contrast, specifying "Write a 300-word blog post for non-technical readers on how generative AI is transforming healthcare, with examples of drug discovery and synthetic data" sets clear expectations about the topic, target audience, and desired length and focus.

**Clarity** is the next critical component. Clear instructions are like a well-written recipe—they reduce ambiguity and increase the likelihood of success. For example, instead of saying, "Write about technology," you might say, "Write about how generative AI can create educational tools, such as quizzes and interactive lessons, for teachers in underserved communities." Clarity supports AI in producing precise and meaningful responses.

**Refinement** involves iterative improvement of prompts to get closer to the desired output. Here's a practical demonstration of refinement:

- *Initial prompt:* "Write a blog post on generative AI in healthcare."
- *AI output:* A generic overview with no clear structure or audience focus.
- *Refined prompt:* "Write a 300-word blog post for non-technical readers on how generative AI accelerates drug discovery."
- *AI output:* A focused response but lacking examples.
- *Final prompt:* "Write a 300-word blog post for non-technical readers on how generative AI accelerates drug discovery, including the design of molecules and the use of synthetic data."
- *AI output:* A polished, example-driven piece tailored to the audience.

This progression demonstrates how context, clarity, and refinement combine to transform a vague prompt into an effective one.

### Method 2: Role, Objective, Limits, and Examples

The role, objective, limits, and examples, or ROLE methodology, makes prompts contextually aware and actionable. Assigning a **role** to the AI helps frame its responses. For instance, you could tell the AI to "act as a branding expert," which sets the stage for creative marketing insights. Defining an **objective** sharpens the focus, such as requesting a "tagline for an eco-friendly laundry detergent."

**Limits** provide constraints that narrow the scope of the response. For example, specifying that the tagline must be "under ten words" encourages concise, impactful results. Finally, **examples** guide the AI by illustrating the style or approach you are aiming for. Here is an illustrative example of this methodology:

- *Prompt:* "Act as a branding expert. Generate a tagline under ten words for an eco-friendly laundry detergent. For inspiration, think of taglines like 'Got Milk?' or 'Just do it' that are memorable and concise."
- *AI output:* "Clean Earth. Clean Clothes. Eco-Friendly Every Day."

This example highlights how ROLE ensures that every element —role, objective, limits, and examples—aligns to produce a focused, relevant response. It is particularly effective for tasks requiring creativity and precision, such as developing marketing materials or product descriptions.

### Method 3: Purpose, Input, Expected Output

The purpose, input, expected output, or PIE methodology, offers a clear and well-structured framework. Start with the **purpose** of the prompt. For example, the purpose might be to "explain generative AI's impact on education to a general audience." Next, provide the **input** necessary for the AI to complete the task effectively. This might include information like "focus on adaptive learning applications and avoid technical jargon."

Finally, specify the **expected output** to help the response align with your goals. For example, you might request a "300-word explanation in a conversational tone." Here's how this methodology plays out:

- *Prompt:* "Explain how generative AI enhances education. Focus on adaptive learning platforms that create personalized lesson plans based on student progress. Write in a conversational tone for a general audience, keeping the response under 300 words."
- *AI output:* A concise, audience-appropriate explanation emphasizing adaptive learning platforms and personalized education.

By adhering to PIE, the AI delivers well-aligned outputs with the specified purpose, input, and expected outcome, ensuring relevance and clarity.

### Method 4: Iterative Feedback and Refinement Loop

The iterative feedback and refinement loop, or IFRL methodology, is a dynamic and collaborative approach to prompt engineering that emphasizes the value of continuous improvement through feedback. Unlike one-off methods, IFRL recognizes that the first attempt at crafting a prompt may yield only a few perfect results. This methodology involves a cycle of feedback, refinement, and reassessment, allowing the user to work closely with the AI to achieve the desired output. The example below demonstrates how this methodology can be put into practice.

- *Step one: Craft the initial prompt.* Begin by creating a prompt that outlines the task at a high level. For example, "Write a 500-word article on renewable energy innovations."

While this provides a general direction, it lacks the specificity required for high-quality results.

- *Step two: Evaluate the AI's output.* Review the AI's response to identify strengths and weaknesses.

In this example, the AI might provide a broad overview but fail to focus on solar energy or include relevant innovations like Tesla's solar roof.

- *Step three: Refine the prompt.* Incorporate feedback into the next iteration of the prompt. For example, a refined version might read: "Write a formal, 500-word article focusing on solar energy innovations, including Tesla's solar roof and community solar projects in the US Midwest."

This updated prompt provides more detail, narrows the focus, and sets clear expectations for tone and content.

- *Step four: Reassess and finalize.* After receiving the revised output, evaluate its alignment with your goals. If further adjustments are needed, continue the loop.

For example, you might refine the tone further by specifying: "Write a formal, 500-word article suitable for publication on a well-renowned renewable energy blog, focusing on solar energy innovations like Tesla's solar roof and community solar projects in the US Midwest, and include statistics to support the benefits of these innovations."

This methodology is particularly effective for complex or nuanced tasks, where initial attempts may only capture some necessary details. By engaging in this iterative process, you will develop a deeper understanding of how best to communicate with generative AI, cultivating a collaborative relationship that enhances the quality of outputs.

The strength of the IFRL methodology lies in its adaptability. Regardless of your request, it guarantees that the final output is polished, precise, and aligned with your objectives. It also reinforces the importance of user oversight, ensuring that AI-generated content meets the highest standards of quality and relevance.

## KEY TAKEAWAY

The CCR, ROLE, PIE, and IFRL methodologies provide powerful frameworks for crafting effective prompts. By practicing and refining these techniques, you'll improve the clarity and adaptability of your prompts and gain a deeper understanding of how to guide AI toward more accurate, insightful, and valuable outputs. Learning these strategies will give you a significant advantage in leveraging generative AI for problem-solving, creativity, and innovation. The more you experiment, the better you will be at harnessing AI to enhance your work and ideas.

# PART 2: MORE ADVANCED PROMPT ENGINEERING

## BREAK DOWN COMPLEX TASKS

One of the most common expert tips is approaching complex scenarios as a series of smaller, interconnected tasks. Instead of presenting the AI with a single, lengthy prompt, splitting the task into manageable pieces to guide the AI step-by-step is often more effective. This modular approach mimics assembling a puzzle, where each piece fits into a larger framework. In practice, if you want the AI to draft a comprehensive report, you might first ask it to outline the main sections, generate content for each section individually, and finally synthesize the content into a cohesive whole. Breaking down tasks in this way supports the AI in maintaining accuracy and clarity, even in intricate workflows. This strategy is beneficial in fields like project management, research, or writing, where nuanced deliverables require incremental progress.

## USE VIVID CONTEXTS FOR CREATIVITY

Use detailed and vivid prompts to unlock the creative potential of generative AI. For example, the AI responds more effectively in creative writing and storytelling when provided with rich scenarios or character descriptions. Rather than asking for a generic story about "a hero saving a kingdom," you might provide a detailed setup: "Write a story about a young alchemist in a desert city who discovers a mysterious potion. Describe how their discovery changes the city and challenges their beliefs about magic." This specificity inspires the AI to generate deeply engaging and imaginative narratives. Similarly, prompts that provide precise contexts, such as market conditions or user personas, help AI produce more targeted and actionable insights in business settings.

This principle extends beyond text generation. Using vivid, detailed language in prompts also enhances AI-generated images, leading to more precise and visually compelling results.

## USE PROMPT CHAINING FOR NUANCED INTERACTIONS

Prompt chaining is a sophisticated technique that allows users to guide AI through a sequence of logically connected tasks, creating an integrated conversation. The AI can reference previous responses by structuring prompts in a chain, building on its earlier outputs to generate more nuanced and context-aware results. For instance, in a scenario involving strategic planning, you could begin by asking the AI to list potential goals for a project. In the following prompt, you might refine those goals by asking, "Based on this list, prioritize the top three goals and provide reasons for each choice." The next prompt could involve asking the AI to create an implementation plan based on the prioritized goals. This technique is especially valuable in education, research, and long-term planning, where tasks are interdependent. Prompt chaining elevates the AI's role from a reactive system to an active partner capable of maintaining coherence across complex workflows.

## IMPROVE AI WITH FEEDBACK LOOPS

A key component of advanced prompt engineering is using feedback loops to refine AI responses over time. Feedback loops involve evaluating the AI's output, identifying areas for improvement, and adjusting future prompts accordingly. This iterative process helps the AI continue learning and adapting, producing higher-quality responses. For example, if an AI-generated marketing campaign lacks specificity, you could revise the prompt to include more explicit instructions, such as "Focus on targeting a younger demographic—between the ages of 18 and 25—interested in sustainable fashion." Feedback loops are particularly effective in dynamic environments where requirements evolve, such as data analysis or customer service. Regularly analyzing prompts' effectiveness and tweaking them based on real-time results can optimize the AI's performance and your overall workflow. This iterative approach transforms prompt engineering into a dynamic practice that evolves alongside the AI's capabilities.

## FINE-TUNE OUTPUTS WITH SYSTEM AND USER PROMPTS

Generative AI systems often operate with two types of input: system prompts and user prompts. System prompts define the AI's overall behavior and tone, while user prompts guide it toward specific outputs. Experts suggest experimenting with both to refine results. For instance, in a customer service application, the system prompt might instruct the AI to respond professionally and empathetically, while user prompts provide details about the specific issue. Combining these inputs allows greater control over the AI's tone and content. For creative writing, a system prompt might set the tone as "lighthearted and humorous," while a user prompt introduces a scenario: "Write a dialogue between two astronauts who accidentally land on an alien planet." By balancing these layers of instruction, you can tailor the AI's responses to meet your needs.

## ADJUST SETTINGS FOR CREATIVITY AND LENGTH

Another more advanced tip is to use 'temperature' and 'token' limits to control the creativity and length of the AI's outputs. Temperature settings control the randomness of the AI's responses. A lower temperature generates more deterministic and predictable results, while a higher temperature encourages creativity and exploration. For instance, in a technical writing context, a temperature of 0.2 might promote factual accuracy, while a setting of 0.8 could inspire more imaginative content for brainstorming sessions. Token limits, on the other hand, determine the length of the AI's response. Setting an appropriate token limit helps maintain a concise and relevant output. For example, when drafting a press release, you might use a limit that keeps the content on a single page. Adjusting these parameters allows users to strike a balance between precision and creativity.

A relatable example to further illustrate this concept is asking AI to devise a joke. You might set the temperature high (0.8 or 0.9) so the AI gets creative and silly. You might also set the token limit low (50 or lower), so the joke is short and to the point. The result might be something like this: "Why don't skeletons fight each other? They don't have the guts!"

## BLEND HUMAN INTUITION WITH AI

Crafting effective prompts goes beyond technical precision; an intuitive grasp of how AI "thinks," and processes language is also vital. Experiment with phrasing, tone, and structure, paying close attention to how subtle changes influence the AI's output. For instance, rephrasing "Explain the effects of smog on human health" as "Write an engaging article for middle school students about how air pollution can affect their health" can result in vastly different responses. This human intuition complements the AI's analytical strengths, ensuring the prompts align closely with the desired outcomes.

* * *

## CHAPTER 4 SELF-ASSESSMENT

It is time to test your knowledge! The QR code and the following shortened link will take you to the end-of-chapter quiz: [**https://tinyurl.com/GenAI-Ch4-Quiz**].

QR code to access the Chapter 4 quiz.

# FIVE
# EXPLORATION OF GENERATIVE AI

When thoughtfully applied, generative AI can streamline complex processes, expand creative possibilities, and tackle challenges with remarkable efficiency. But when things go wrong, they can go very wrong, with errors that range from embarrassing to catastrophic. This chapter explores both sides of the spectrum—showcasing AI at its most brilliant and most flawed—to demonstrate the difference between success and failure in generative AI.

## WHEN THINGS GO RIGHT, THEY GO VERY, VERY RIGHT...

### Malaria No More: AI-Powered Global Awareness

In 2019, Malaria No More launched its "Malaria Must Die" campaign, using generative AI to amplify its message worldwide. The campaign featured a video of David Beckham speaking nine languages, which was made possible by Synthesia's AI video synthesis technology. AI mapped Beckham's facial expressions and mouth movements to match native speakers' recordings, allowing the message to reach diverse audiences.

The video gained over 700 million digital impressions and helped Malaria No More secure $4 billion in funding, with support from organizations like the Bill and Melinda Gates Foundation. This campaign highlights how generative AI can break language barriers, expand global reach, and drive meaningful action in public health initiatives.

### Shopify's Approach to Empowering Merchants

Shopify integrates generative AI into its platform to help merchants create content more efficiently and optimize their online stores. Through its "Shopify Magic" suite, sellers can generate product descriptions, marketing copy, and even AI-enhanced images to create higher-quality listings to better attract customers. The AI tools analyze product details and generate compelling, SEO-friendly descriptions in seconds, reducing the time merchants spend on manual content creation.

Beyond content generation, Shopify's AI capabilities assist with inventory management and customer engagement, providing personalized insights to help businesses operate more efficiently. These AI-powered enhancements have contributed to Shopify's continued growth, particularly in helping small and medium-sized businesses compete in the evolving e-commerce landscape. By integrating generative AI into its ecosystem, Shopify enables merchants to scale their businesses with less effort while maintaining high-quality, engaging storefronts.

### Octopus Energy Transforming Customer Service

Octopus Energy, a UK-based renewable energy provider, has integrated generative AI into its customer service operations, significantly improving efficiency. By mid-2023, AI systems were handling over one-third of all customer emails, performing the equivalent workload of 250 human agents. This automation has led to faster response times while maintaining the company's reputation for strong customer engagement.

AI-generated responses have also achieved an 80% customer satisfaction rate, surpassing human-generated responses. This success stems from AI's ability to analyze previous interactions, craft consistent, well-structured replies, and use empathetic language tailored to individual customers. By streamlining routine inquiries, the AI allows human agents to focus on complex cases, ensuring a seamless experience for customers who need personalized assistance.

### Key Takeaway

These examples demonstrate generative AI's immense potential to enhance creativity, efficiency, and problem-solving across various fields. They also show that the technology is most impactful when thoughtfully applied to address specific challenges and aligned with real-world needs. The key lesson is that successful implementation requires technical expertise, a clear understanding of the problem, careful integration into workflows, and a commitment to achieving meaningful outcomes.

## ...BUT WHEN THINGS GO WRONG, THEY GO HORRIBLY WRONG

### DPD's Chatbot Misstep

DPD, a delivery company, faced a notable incident in which its AI-powered chatbot swore at a customer. A frustrated customer unable to track a parcel manipulated the chatbot into generating inappropriate responses, including swearing and mocking poems about the company. This exchange went viral on social media, exposing the chatbot's vulnerability to prompt manipulation and raising concerns about its effectiveness in customer service. DPD responded by temporarily disabling the AI component, attributing the issue to a recent system update.

## DoNotPay's Untested Robot Lawyer

DoNotPay, which markets itself as the "world's first robot lawyer," offers AI-driven services such as contesting parking tickets and handling minor legal issues. However, in September 2024, the company faced significant legal challenges when the U.S. Federal Trade Commission (FTC) fined it $193,000 for deceptive advertising claims. The FTC found that DoNotPay falsely exaggerated its AI capabilities, leading customers to believe the platform provided more advanced legal assistance than it could deliver.

This incident raised concerns about the accountability and transparency of AI applications in legal services. It also highlighted the risks of overpromising AI capabilities without adequate safeguards or transparency. DoNotPay's case underscores the importance of ensuring that AI-driven services meet advertised standards and the consequences of failing in a highly regulated sector like legal services.

## OpenAI's Sora Leak

OpenAI's video-generation tool, Sora, was leaked by artists protesting the program's rollout and minimal compensation. The leak allowed public access to the AI, leading to unauthorized video creations. Artists accused OpenAI of exploiting their unpaid labor during Sora's early testing phase, known as "red teaming." In response, OpenAI quickly revoked early access and emphasized that Sora was still in research preview. This incident underscores the importance of clear communication and fair compensation when involving external contributors in AI development.

## Lessons Learned

These cases illustrate the critical importance of thorough testing, robust prompt engineering, and ethical considerations in AI deployment. Ensuring that AI systems are resilient to manipulation, accurately trained, and ethically managed is essential to prevent costly failures and maintain public trust.

* * *

## CHAPTER 5 SELF-ASSESSMENT

Solidify your understanding of this Chapter by taking the short end-of-chapter self-assessment quiz. To get started, simply scan the QR code or go to [**https://tinyurl.com/GenAI-Ch5-Quiz**].

QR code to access the Chapter 5 quiz.

# SIX

# THE EVOLUTION OF PROMPT ENGINEERING AND NOTABLE CONTRIBUTORS TO THE FIELD

Prompt engineering has evolved into a pivotal discipline, driven by the contributions of diverse figures and groundbreaking technological advancements. The roots of this field can be traced back to the 1960s when Joseph Weizenbaum at MIT developed ELIZA, an early natural language processing program that simulated conversation by identifying keywords and generating context-appropriate responses. ELIZA underscored the importance of structuring inputs to guide AI outputs, laying the groundwork for what we now recognize as prompt engineering.

In the following decades, AI research advanced significantly, moving from rule-based approaches to statistical methods and eventually to deep learning. The introduction of neural networks and transformer architectures, particularly Google's BERT (now Gemini) in 2018 and OpenAI's GPT series, marked a transformative era in natural language processing. OpenAI released GPT-3 in 2020, followed by GPT-3.5 in 2022, which powered ChatGPT's initial version, launched in November 2022. GPT-4, released in March 2023, further emphasized the necessity of prompt engineering, as these models demonstrated an unprecedented ability to generate meaningful and accurate responses—provided that users crafted well-structured prompts. Subsequent advancements further reshaped the landscape of AI capabilities. In May 2024, OpenAI launched GPT-4o ("o" for "omni"), a multilingual, multimodal model capable of processing and generating text, images, and audio. This iteration brought faster response times and significant improvements in task performance, highlighting OpenAI's focus on creating versatile AI systems. Shortly after, in July 2024, OpenAI introduced GPT-4o Mini, a smaller and more cost-effective version that retained the advanced features of GPT-4o while surpassing GPT-3.5 Turbo in benchmarks.

In September 2024, OpenAI took another leap forward by releasing the o1 model. Designed to enhance reasoning capabilities, o1 marked a departure from models that relied solely on statistical predictions. Instead, it introduced systems capable of "thinking" and solving problems through trial and error, paving the way for AI that more closely mimics human-like reasoning.

Building on this progress, OpenAI announced the o3 model in December 2024. This iteration improved upon o1 by incorporating extended deliberation time for complex, step-by-step logical reasoning. This refinement allowed o3 to break down intricate problems into more manageable components, significantly increasing accuracy and reliability. Notably, o3 achieved a 71.7% accuracy on the SWE-Bench Verified coding benchmark,* surpassing o1 by over 20%. Alongside the full o3 model, OpenAI introduced o3-Mini, a lighter and more efficient version that retains the reasoning enhancements of o3 while reducing computational costs, making it a more accessible option for developers and businesses.

---

* The SWE-Bench Verified benchmark measures how well AI models can understand and fix real coding problems. It is based on software issues from GitHub, where developers collaborate on code. The "Verified" version includes 500 coding problems that experts have checked to ensure they are realistic and solvable. AI models are given these problems and asked to generate fixes, similar to how a human programmer would debug code.

OpenAI's o3 model achieved 71.7% accuracy on this benchmark, meaning it successfully fixed about 72 out of every 100 coding issues it was given. This represents a significant improvement over its predecessor, o1, showing that o3 is significantly better at identifying and correcting real-world software problems.

In January 2025, OpenAI unveiled "Operator," an AI agent designed to autonomously perform web-based tasks by interacting with on-screen elements such as buttons, menus, and text fields. This innovation enables the automation of various activities, including filling out forms, ordering groceries, and creating to-do lists, broadening the practical applications of AI in daily life. Initially released as a research preview for Pro users in the United States, Operator represents a significant step toward integrating AI agents into routine tasks.

Concurrently, the AI landscape witnessed a notable development from China's DeepSeek, which introduced the DeepSeek-R1 model. This open-source reasoning model has demonstrated performance comparable to OpenAI's o1 model and, in some cases, matching or surpassing the o3 model in areas such as mathematics, coding, and natural language reasoning. Remarkably, DeepSeek-R1 was developed with significantly lower computational resources and costs, utilizing only about 2,000 specialized computer chips and approximately $5.6 million for training. This efficiency challenges the prevailing notion that advanced AI development necessitates extensive resources, highlighting the potential for more cost-effective approaches.

The rapid advancements in AI have not only transformed technology but have also reshaped how experts conceptualize and interact with these systems. Scholars and practitioners from diverse fields have emphasized the significance of prompt engineering in guiding AI models toward producing relevant and practical outputs. Barbara J. Grosz, a computer scientist at Harvard University, advanced the understanding of natural language communication between humans and machines, establishing principles that directly influenced how modern AI systems process and generate text. In a 2015 interview on her work to make human-computer interactions more fluent, she said,

> *We knew that if we were going to have a system that could carry on a dialogue and be able to handle the way people actually spoke, we needed to have a computational model of dialogue that could track context.*

Similarly, Ethan Mollick at the University of Pennsylvania's Wharton School has highlighted the practical applications of prompt engineering in education and business, advising leaders on integrating AI responsibly while leveraging the power of prompts to maximize value. Albert Phelps, a prompt engineer at Mudano, described this skill as essential in the era of generative AI, noting its increasing demand in both technical and creative fields.

Catherine Havasi, co-founder of Luminoso, contributed significantly to AI's contextual understanding through her work on ConceptNet, an open-source knowledge graph that helps language models interpret nuanced language. Her contributions underscore the importance of context in effective prompt engineering. Aras Bozkurt of Anadolu University expanded the field's conceptualization, framing it as both an art and a science, emphasizing the interdisciplinary nature of designing effective prompts. In parallel, Anna Korhonen, a linguistics and AI researcher at the University of Cambridge, has advanced tools that bridge language models with real-world challenges, reinforcing the importance of these systems in solving global problems. Meanwhile, Golam Md Muktadir's publication, *A Brief History of Prompt: Leveraging Language Models Through Advanced Prompting*, offers a comprehensive historical exploration of the field, documenting its evolution and highlighting its critical role in AI development.

The evolution of prompt engineering reflects the broader development of AI systems, transitioning from simple rule-based interactions to nuanced dialogues. Generative AI tools today owe much of their sophistication to early systems like ELIZA and the computational leaps made possible by neural networks and transformer architectures. The field has become a bridge between human creativity and machine intelligence, enabling applications across industries ranging from education to business to healthcare.

These advancements underscore the extremely rapid evolution of AI technologies and the increasing global contributions to the field. The emergence of efficient models like DeepSeek-R1, combined with OpenAI's continual improvements in reasoning and automation with models like o3 and Operator, intensifies competition and encourages innovation. I suspect we will see other companies begin to feverishly release their new models to keep up (or at least not have the gap widened) with the leaders in this space. As AI systems become more powerful and cost-efficient, they will continue transforming industries and expanding their accessibility, soon setting the stage for even more significant breakthroughs.

This historical journey, enriched by the contributions of innovators across disciplines and perspectives, has positioned prompt engineering as a cornerstone of AI's practical applications. As AI continues to evolve, prompt engineering will remain a critical skill, allowing users to unlock the full potential of these robust systems.

* * *

## CHAPTER 6 SELF-ASSESSMENT

Try the short quiz to test your knowledge of this chapter. Scan the QR code below or enter the following URL into your browser: [**https://tinyurl.com/GenAI-Ch6-Quiz**].

QR code to access the Chapter 6 quiz.

SEVEN
# GENERATIVE AI BEYOND THE BASICS

This chapter will explore more advanced topics in generative AI and cutting-edge tools and technologies, such as quantum computing and edge AI. We will see how these technologies amplify generative AI's capabilities and how they combine with techniques to enable these models to be efficient, impactful, and ethical.

## RETRIEVAL-AUGMENTED GENERATION

Combing through documents to find that one crucial piece of information or sifting through overwhelming data to identify trends is a challenge many of us have faced. This is where retrieval-augmented generation (RAG) excels. By combining the precision of retrieval systems with the creativity of generative models, RAG doesn't just locate relevant information—it synthesizes it into concise, insightful summaries tailored to your needs. Think of RAG as an expert librarian who finds the most relevant books, reads through them, extracts the key points, and provides a summary perfectly aligned to your research needs or queries.

So, how exactly does RAG achieve this? RAG integrates real-time data from external sources, such as databases, APIs, or indexed repositories. For example, RAG can access product manuals or troubleshooting guides in a customer support system in real-time, generating precise and context-aware responses to customer queries. In the context of academic research, RAG can pull from vast online libraries to synthesize findings or provide detailed explanations.

"Search meets Creativity," generated by DALL-E and edited in Canva.

Unlike static models that rely solely on preexisting training data, RAG dynamically retrieves the most relevant, up-to-date information. This helps keep its responses grounded in the latest knowledge. This is especially important in fields such as healthcare, where access to current studies and guidelines impacts decision-making, or in legal settings, where staying informed about recent legislation is imperative.

RAG seamlessly integrates retrieval and generation. Its workflow is as follows: First, advanced retrieval techniques identify the most relevant data sources. Second, generative capabilities create coherent, context-enriched responses tailored to the user's query. Finally, accurate and nuanced responses are produced, including depth and detail critical for effective decision-making or problem-solving. With RAG, information overload is translated into actionable knowledge.

However, there are challenges with implementing RAG. One such challenge is ensuring data relevance and accuracy. With vast information sources, distinguishing between high-quality and unreliable data requires robust algorithms that assess source credibility and refine model performance. Another challenge is optimizing retrieval efficiency, as large data volumes can create bottlenecks, slowing retrieval.

## MULTIMODAL AI

Multimodal AI is a significant advancement in artificial intelligence. As we learned in Chapter 2, multimodal AI integrates various data types—such as text, images, and audio—to create richer, more nuanced interactions. Unlike single modality systems, which rely on a single input type, multimodal AI combines and synthesizes information from multiple formats, enabling AI systems to better understand context and deliver more intuitive and human-like responses. For example, a multimodal AI system can interpret a spoken question (audio), cross-reference related visuals (images), and generate a detailed textual response, all in a seamless workflow.

One of the main hurdles in effectively implementing multimodal AI is synchronizing disparate data streams, each with its own structures and processing requirements. Aligning these modes requires advanced algorithms capable of harmonizing inputs in real-time to achieve seamless interpretation and synthesis. Computational efficiency is another factor, as the simultaneous processing of multimodal inputs typically requires immense computational power.

Technological frameworks are crucial in advancing multimodal AI, providing the tools and infrastructure required to integrate and process varied data types. Platforms like TensorFlow and PyTorch have emerged as key enablers of multimodal AI systems as they facilitate seamless data integration, enabling developers to create AI systems that adapt dynamically to diverse inputs. Specialized APIs further enhance this capability, allowing real-time interaction between data streams.

### Contextual Information from a Smartphone Camera

Google Lens is a prime example of multimodal AI at work. It integrates visual and textual modalities to provide contextual information based on what the user captures with their smartphone's camera. For instance, pointing the lens at a restaurant sign brings up reviews, menus, and directions. Similarly, if a user scans text in a foreign language, Google Lens can translate it in real-time and even read it aloud, combining visual, textual, and auditory processing for a holistic user experience.

I regularly use an app called PictureThis – Plant Identifier that works similarly to Google Lens. I go garden spotting regularly when I am out and about. When I see a shrub, a tree, or flower that I like, or when I encounter cool-looking moss (I have a quiet affection for these slow-growing bryophytes—their resilience, intricate textures, and hidden ecosystems—much like Alma Whittaker in *The Signature of All Things)* I open my app and point my camera to the plant in question, and it tells me exactly what it is, its native habitat, whether or not it's invasive, how much sun or shade it likes, how to take care of it, and more. I have a garden full of plants that I've documented using this app. I also use the Picture This app when hiking with my light-hearted pup Züri, who likes to put everything in her mouth. I can quickly identify mushrooms or other toxic plants to steer clear of.

"Smartphone analyzing mushroom for toxicity," generated by DALL-E from text prompts. Edited in Canva.

## Diagnostic Precision

In healthcare, multimodal AI elevates diagnostic precision by combining diverse data streams such as medical imaging, patient histories, and vocal biomarkers. This comprehensive approach allows healthcare providers to generate holistic insights, which improve diagnostics and treatment outcomes.

## Virtual Assistants

Meanwhile, in consumer technology, virtual assistants such as Google Assistant, Samsung's Bixby, and Perplexity AI Assistant have evolved into sophisticated multimodal entities. They respond to voice commands and accompanying visual cues, such as pointing to an object and asking about it. By uniting these modalities, they deliver contextually enriched responses tailored to individual user needs.

### Interactive Media

In entertainment, multimodal AI redefines interactive media, enabling experiences that adapt dynamically to user inputs across multiple sensory channels. For example, films can now adjust their storylines in real time based on audience reactions detected through facial expression analysis to enhance immersion and personalization. *Lilith.Aeon*, the world's first AI-driven dance production, brings responsive elements to live performances, while Meta's Movie Gen generates video and audio that adapt to user prompts. These advancements empower creators to craft deeply engaging narratives that seamlessly blend visuals, sound, and interactivity.

## GENERATIVE AI MEETS QUANTUM COMPUTING

Quantum computing offers new ways to solve complex problems beyond traditional computers' capabilities. Leveraging quantum bits (qubits), which can exist in multiple states simultaneously—referred to as superposition—quantum systems can process vast amounts of data with extraordinary speed. When quantum computing is paired with generative AI, the innovation potential expands significantly.

### Drug Discovery

Pharmaceutical companies and collaborations are increasingly exploring quantum computing to revolutionize drug discovery. For instance, Quantinuum, formed from the merger of Cambridge Quantum and Honeywell Quantum Solutions, is developing quantum computing solutions aimed at enhancing drug discovery and delivery processes.

IBM, through its IBM Q Network, is also investigating how quantum computing can accelerate drug discovery. Their research focuses on modeling complex molecular structures with high precision, which is crucial for developing new pharmaceuticals.

By combining quantum computing with generative AI, these systems can simulate molecular behaviors and stability, suggesting potential drug candidates more efficiently than traditional methods. While fully integrated workflows are still under development, researchers anticipate that these tools will expedite the identification of molecules capable of inhibiting diseases like cancer, streamlining the drug discovery process.

### Material Science

BMW Group is investigating quantum computing applications to accelerate research into sustainable vehicles. By integrating generative AI with quantum systems, the company is exploring novel materials for lighter, more energy-efficient cars. AI can propose material compositions based on sustainability and performance criteria, while quantum computing simulates their physical and chemical properties. This approach has the potential to identify materials that reduce environmental impact and enhance vehicle performance, though many applications are still in the experimental phases.

### Chemical Reactions and Novel Compounds

BASF, a leading chemical company, is actively exploring quantum computing and generative AI to accelerate materials discovery and chemical reaction predictions. Generative AI assists in suggesting potential formulations, while quantum computing is being tested for simulating complex chemical reactions, such as those in homogeneous catalysis. BASF has partnered with companies like SEEQC and Zapata Computing to advance these capabilities. In agriculture, BASF is leveraging generative AI, such as in its xarvio® FIELD MANAGER platform, to provide data-driven agronomic advice. While these technologies hold great promise for designing novel compounds, optimizing fertilizers, and improving pesticide formulations, their full-scale industrial application remains a work in progress.

## EDGE AI

Edge AI refers to artificial intelligence that runs directly on local devices instead of relying on cloud servers. This means AI-powered tasks—like speech recognition, image processing, or real-time decision-making—happen on smartphones, cameras, sensors, or other edge devices without needing to send data to a distant server.

Edge AI provides several key advantages: It reduces lag time, enhances privacy by keeping data local, and allows AI to function even without an internet connection. Edge AI is commonly used in smart assistants, self-driving cars, industrial automation, and security systems.

### Retail Checkout Systems

Amazon's Just Walk Out technology is a leading example of Edge AI in autonomous retail checkout systems. While this system currently uses Edge AI to track purchases and automate payments, generative AI could expand its capabilities in the future. For example, generative AI could dynamically create personalized product recommendations or promotional offers based on in-store customer behavior. These actions would happen locally, ensuring both speed and privacy, though such applications remain largely aspirational at this stage.

### Smart Manufacturing

Siemens is integrating Edge AI into its industrial automation solutions to optimize production processes by enabling real-time data processing directly on the factory floor. The Siemens Industrial Copilot, a generative AI-powered assistant, enhances automation by generating code, supporting visualization, and providing operational recommendations. While pairing Edge AI with generative AI opens new possibilities, full automation—where machines autonomously detect quality fluctuations and AI simulates fixes without cloud reliance—is still evolving. However, these advancements aim to minimize downtime, improve product consistency, and enhance overall efficiency in industrial settings.

## OPTIMIZING GENERATIVE AI MODELS FOR PERFORMANCE AND PRIVACY

Optimizing generative AI models involves advanced techniques that make them faster, more efficient, and adaptable to complex scenarios. Pruning and quantization, for instance, streamline generative AI models by reducing unnecessary computational layers, ensuring they remain efficient while maintaining creative output quality.

Federated learning adds another dimension to generative AI by allowing models to train on decentralized data sources without compromising privacy.

### Pruning and Quantization

Optimization techniques like pruning and quantization have become essential for making cutting-edge AI tools accessible and efficient. Companies such as Runway ML, a platform for creators to generate high-resolution images and videos using AI, and OpenAI's DALL-E employ these methods to deliver high-performance AI applications without requiring users to invest in expensive hardware.

For example, Runway ML enables users to produce high-resolution visual content on devices with standard processing capabilities, eliminating the need for high-end GPUs. This is accomplished through pruning, which involves removing redundant or less critical neural connections in the AI model, and quantization, which reduces the precision of model parameters while maintaining accuracy. Together, these techniques significantly lower the computational load, making complex AI tasks feasible on consumer-grade devices.

Similarly, OpenAI's DALL-E streamlines its underlying architecture through pruning and quantization, enabling rapid image generation without compromising creativity or fidelity. These optimizations also allow for the deployment of such tools in web-based environments and mobile applications, extending their accessibility to a broader audience.

Beyond enhancing efficiency, pruning and quantization also contribute to sustainability by reducing the energy consumption required for AI model training and inference.

The broader implication of these techniques is the democratization of AI. By enabling advanced tools to run effectively on less powerful hardware, companies like Runway ML and OpenAI are lowering barriers to entry for creators, developers, and researchers, promoting innovation across diverse fields.

**Federated Learning**

Federated learning allows organizations to collaborate in a 'closed-loop system,' enabling the development of robust, shared machine learning models without the need to exchange data directly. This approach maintains data privacy while encouraging innovation across industries.

Companies like Google have successfully implemented federated learning to train AI models on decentralized data. For example, Google's Gboard keyboard uses federated learning to enhance text and emoji predictions by training directly on user data stored on devices. This ensures that sensitive information, such as typing patterns, remains on the user's phone, preserving privacy while improving functionality.

In healthcare, federated learning is being explored by initiatives such as Owkin, which applies AI models to analyze medical data across institutions while keeping patient records localized. This enables the generation of insights into treatments and disease patterns without compromising patient privacy or violating regulations like the United States Health Insurance Portability and Accountability Act (HIPAA) and the European Union's General Data Protection Regulation (GDPR).

Platforms like NVIDIA Clara integrate federated learning alongside techniques for generating synthetic medical data to train AI systems. For example, Clara creates simulated MRI scans for training models to detect anomalies. These synthetic datasets allow healthcare providers to improve diagnostic accuracy while adhering to strict privacy requirements.

In addition, Canva, a popular design tool, incorporates lightweight generative AI features, such as automated image creation and text-to-image capabilities. By optimizing models with techniques like pruning and quantization, Canva enables these features to run efficiently in web-based environments, making them accessible to millions of users worldwide, even on devices with limited processing power.

* * *

## CHAPTER 7 SELF-ASSESSMENT

Challenge yourself with a quick quiz. To access it, either scan the QR code below or enter **[https://tinyurl.com/GenAI-Ch7-Quiz]** into your browser.

QR code to access the Chapter 7 quiz.

# MAKE A DIFFERENCE WITH YOUR REVIEW

Help others unlock the power of generative AI for productivity, creativity, and career success!

*"No act of kindness, no matter how small, is ever wasted."* – Aesop

A few words can go a long way.

Would you help someone take their first step into generative AI? By sharing your thoughts, you're guiding others in deciding if this book is right for them. Your review could inspire:

...a business owner to boost productivity and innovation with AI.
...a writer to enhance their craft with AI-assisted storytelling.
...a musician to compose and produce with AI-driven tools.
...an entrepreneur to turn ideas into reality faster with AI.
...a professional to gain a competitive edge in their field.
...a lifelong learner to unlock new creative and career opportunities.

*Leaving a review takes less than a minute but leaves a lasting impact!*

QR code to leave a review. URL:
**https://geni.us/GenAIReviewPB**

# EIGHT
# ETHICAL CONSIDERATIONS AND SOCIAL IMPLICATIONS

> New technology is not good or evil in and of itself. It's all about how people choose to use it.
>
> DAVID WONG (JASON PARGIN), AUTHOR AND SOCIAL COMMENTATOR ON TECHNOLOGY AND CULTURE

While generative AI has emerged as one of the most transformative technologies of our time, its capabilities do come with unique ethical concerns that demand careful attention. Addressing these challenges is critical to ensuring this technology is deployed responsibly and equitably, maximizing its benefits, and minimizing risks. In this chapter, we will explore several ethical considerations for generative AI and the social implications associated with its use. We'll also explore various mitigation measures to combat these ethical and social consequences.

## MISINFORMATION AND DEEPFAKES

A deepfake is synthetic media created using AI techniques, specifically deep learning. It involves manipulating or generating audio, video, or images to make them appear real. Deepfakes often depict someone doing or saying something they never actually did. The term is derived from "deep learning" and "fake."

Generative AI's capacity for creating hyper-realistic content has fueled misinformation campaigns globally. A well-known example is the use of AI-generated videos in political contexts. In 2018, a lifetime ago in the world of tech, a deepfake video of former U.S. President Obama emerged, in which he appeared to make statements he never actually said. Although filmmaker Jordan Peele and Buzzfeed created this video to raise awareness about deepfake risks, the technology continues to be exploited to spread false narratives, erode trust in leadership, and destabilize elections.

Another notable and recent AI-generated video, "This is Not Morgan Freeman – A Deepfake Singularity" by Diep Nep on YouTube, is incredibly realistic and worth watching.

Captured image from Diep Nep's video, "This is not Morgan Freeman - A Deepfake Singularity," on YouTube. Edited in Canva. Watch the video: [**https://tinyurl.com/ThisisnotMorganFreeman**]

Diep Nep has also shared "This is Not Morgan Freeman – A Look Behind the Deepfake Singularity," which provides an insightful glimpse into the technology behind it. While these videos are impressive, the quality of AI-generated videos has advanced even further since their creation, making it increasingly challenging to distinguish real from fabricated.

Captured image from Diep Nep's video, "This is not Morgan Freeman - A look behind the Deepfake Singularity." Edited in Canva. Watch it here: [**https://tinyurl.com/MorganFreemanBehindTheScenes**]

In May 2024, an alarming incident occurred when Mark Read, CEO of WPP—the world's largest advertising group—was targeted in a sophisticated deepfake scam. Fraudsters cloned Read's voice and used an AI-generated video to impersonate him during a Microsoft Teams meeting, attempting to deceive employees into transferring funds. Although the scam was unsuccessful due to the vigilance of WPP executives, it underscores the growing threat of AI-generated impersonations in corporate settings. This serves as a wake-up call for us all, as it is not only high-powered and well-paid CEOs who are the targets of such cons. Any one of us could fall prey to this sort of scam.

Another example of voice cloning occurred in early 2024, when French DJ David Guetta played a new track featuring Eminem's voice during a live set. The only problem was that Eminem wasn't there and did not, to our knowledge, collaborate with Guetta in the making of this track. AI cloned Eminem's voice. Did Eminem grant permission to Guetta to do this? Did Eminem even have to give consent? I'm sure this will be debated for some time.

## What is Happening to Combat this Rise in Deepfakes?

Thankfully, several efforts and initiatives are underway to mitigate this issue. However, maintaining your vigilance, which we'll explore in greater detail in Chapter 9, will continue to be important.

### ***Organizations are investing in sophisticated detection tools to identify and counter deepfakes.***

The U.S. Department of Defense awarded a $2.4 million contract to Hive AI to develop technologies capable of detecting manipulated video, image, and audio content. Furthermore, companies like Reality Defender and Sensity AI offer platforms that utilize advanced AI algorithms to analyze media, determine its authenticity, and provide detailed reports and visualizations of potential manipulations.

### ***Governments are enacting laws to address the issue of deepfakes.***

In 2023, the U.S. Congress introduced the DEEPFAKES Accountability Act, which aims to impose transparency requirements on creators of synthetic media and establish penalties for misuse. At the state level, California has the United States' most aggressive law; it bans digitally altered political deepfakes and compels platforms to pull down such content when users flag it.

In September 2024, South Korea's National Assembly passed legislation criminalizing the possession and viewing of deepfake pornography! Action against explicit deepfakes was taken due to public outcry about the proliferation of such videos, particularly those shared in Telegram group chats. Individuals found purchasing, saving, or watching such material could face prison time or fines up to 30 million won, or approximately US$22,800.

***Some tech companies and platforms are implementing policies to combat the spread of deepfakes.***

In a global first, TikTok introduced automatic labeling of AI-generated content to inform users about the nature of the media they encounter. Also, in April 2024, Meta implemented "Made with AI" labels on AI-generated images and videos on Facebook, Instagram, and Threads. Visible markers, invisible watermarks, and embedded metadata inform users about the nature of the content they encounter on these platforms. This effort to combat deepfakes remains in place at the time of writing despite other significant policy changes at the company, which I'll touch on later.

***Collaborative initiatives are spurring the development of innovative technologies to detect manipulated media.***

One notable collaborative initiative is the Coalition for Content Provenance and Authenticity, or C2PA. This alliance, which includes Adobe, Microsoft, and the BBC, focuses on developing standards for certifying the source and authenticity of digital media.

The Content Authenticity Initiative (CAI), launched by Adobe in 2019, aims to combat misinformation by developing standards for digital content attribution. Since its inception, the CAI has expanded to include over 2,000 members, encompassing a diverse coalition of technology firms, social media platforms, news organizations, camera manufacturers, and civil society groups. Initial collaborators included The New York Times Company and Twitter before it became "X" after Elon Musk bought it.

## BIAS IN AI-GENERATED OUTPUTS

Bias in generative AI arises when models are trained on datasets that reflect historical prejudices, stereotypes, or unbalanced perspectives. These biases can manifest in harmful ways, such as reinforcing gender stereotypes in job descriptions, generating racially insensitive art, or excluding marginalized groups in creative outputs. For example, an AI system might produce job descriptions that implicitly favor one gender over another for leadership roles. This can have far-reaching societal consequences as AI-generated content is increasingly integrated into hiring, media, and decision-making processes.

To mitigate this, developers must prioritize diversity in training datasets and audit them to identify and remove biases. Incorporating diverse perspectives helps models generate more inclusive outputs and reflect society's breadth. Beyond the training stage, content filters and human oversight can help flag and adjust biased outputs before they reach the public.

## INTELLECTUAL PROPERTY RIGHTS

Generative AI has led to contentious debates around ownership and originality. For instance, when AI art models like DALL-E and Stable Diffusion generated images that bore uncanny resemblances to copyrighted works, many artists claimed their styles had been appropriated without consent. Another notable controversy arose when an AI-generated piece of art titled "Théâtre D'opéra Spatial" by Jason Allen won a digital art competition in 2022, igniting debates about whether AI creations qualify as art and who should claim authorship—is the creator the AI, or is it Allen, the person who provided the prompts? In this instance, the U.S. Copyright Office decided against providing copyright protection for the piece, citing a lack of human authorship. But this isn't the end of the debate; artists not receiving protections for their AI works could have profound implications for the growing field of digital art.

Mitigation measures are being implemented to address these

concerns, including licensing agreements for training data, opt-out mechanisms for creators whose work feeds into AI training datasets, utilizing watermarking and attributions standards, legislation such as the European Union's AI Act, and companies implementing policies ensuring datasets used for AI training are ethically sourced and come with clear documentation about their origins and associated rights.

## OVER-RELIANCE ON GENERATIVE AI

I've already mentioned the concern about overreliance on generative AI a few times. Still, it's worth unpacking this concern further, especially as generative AI tools become more accessible and powerful. There is a growing tendency to overuse them in ways that can backfire. While these tools excel at automating tasks, streamlining workflows, and creating innovative content, overreliance on AI can lead to unintended consequences that undermine trust, authenticity, and effectiveness.

For instance, consider a scenario where a company relies solely on AI to generate its marketing materials. While the AI can produce grammatically correct and visually appealing content, it might miss cultural nuances, resulting in campaigns that feel impersonal or tone-deaf to target audiences. This hypothetical situation could lead to reputational damage and a loss of customer connection, as the content lacks the human touch required to resonate authentically.

Another example might involve a university using AI to draft communications following a campus crisis. Though efficient, the AI's lack of emotional intelligence could produce a message that feels robotic or insensitive to the gravity of the situation. In such cases, the absence of human oversight could amplify tensions rather than ease them, highlighting the need for a balance between automation and empathy.

There is growing concern in education that tools like ChatGPT may hinder learning. Some educators have observed that students who heavily depend on ChatGPT for assignments may experience a decline in their ability to think critically, independently solve problems, and understand the subject matter. A study involving undergraduate students found that prolonged use of ChatGPT for academic tasks could negatively affect their creativity. This research indicates a potential threat to developing original ideas due to dependence on AI-generated content. And then there's the issue of academic integrity: students and educators have raised concerns that using generative tools like ChatGPT could encourage academic dishonesty. These examples highlight the importance of balancing the use of AI tools like ChatGPT with traditional learning methods.

Watercolor cartoon by fine artist Edward Wedler, DTM, ACWA of Bedford, Nova Scotia. To view more of his and his wife's art, visit https://www.wedlerfineart.com/.

## DATA COLLECTION AND PRIVACY VIOLATIONS

Generative AI systems rely heavily on vast data to train and refine their models. While this data is essential for improving performance and accuracy, it often includes sensitive or personal information, raising critical privacy concerns. Without stringent safeguards, AI systems may inadvertently reveal private or sensitive data during training or in response to user queries. Furthermore, many datasets used to train AI models are compiled without explicit consent, raising serious ethical concerns about ownership and privacy. Also, the complexity of generative AI systems can create unforeseen vulnerabilities, such as bugs or gaps in data protection, leading to breaches.

There are several notable examples of generative AI systems breaching privacy and eroding trust in such systems. One such incident occurred when a bug in OpenAI's ChatGPT exposed the titles of users' conversation histories to other users. While the actual content of the chats remained inaccessible, the incident revealed vulnerabilities in how sensitive data is handled. This highlighted the need for stronger measures to ensure user information is securely stored and displayed. In another example from 2023, Samsung employees unknowingly fed confidential data, including internal meeting notes and proprietary source code, into ChatGPT for assistance with work-related tasks. This data was subsequently incorporated into the AI's training process, sparking concerns over intellectual property and data security. In response, Samsung implemented strict policies restricting generative AI tools within its organization, reflecting the growing anxiety around corporate data privacy.

AI voice assistants have also been at the center of privacy concerns. Amazon's Alexa, for example, was criticized when it was revealed that human reviewers had listened to user recordings, some of which captured private conversations inadvertently triggered by the device. While this practice aimed to improve the AI's speech recognition capabilities, it raised questions about the transparency of AI systems and user consent.

Another notable incident highlighting these concerns involved Otter.ai, a transcription service designed to record and transcribe meetings. In October 2024, researcher and engineer Alex Bilzerian recounted an experience where Otter AI continued recording a Zoom meeting even after he had logged off. The AI captured hours of private conversations among venture capitalists, including intimate and confidential business details. This unintentional recording led Bilzerian to terminate a potential deal with the firm, underscoring the unintended consequences of AI technologies in professional settings.

In response to such incidents, companies like Otter.ai have

emphasized their commitment to user privacy, offering features that allow users to control sharing permissions and manage recordings. However, these measures rely heavily on user awareness and proper configuration, which may not always be in place. This situation exemplifies the broader challenges of ensuring privacy in AI applications, where the technology's capabilities can outpace users' understanding and control.

There are, thankfully, various mitigation measures being implemented to address privacy risks, including:

- *Data minimization* is collecting only the information necessary for training AI models. This practice has gained traction in reducing the exposure of sensitive data. Companies such as Stability AI and non-profit organizations such as LAION now provide opt-out mechanisms, allowing individuals and companies to remove their data from training datasets.
- *Differential privacy and encryption* are advanced techniques for anonymizing user information and ensuring it cannot be traced back to specific individuals.
- *Transparency initiatives* like Adobe's Content Authenticity Initiative offer more transparent documentation of data use, giving users a better understanding of how their information is handled.
- *Regulatory frameworks*, such as the European Union's GDPR and the recently adopted EU AI Act, mandate strict controls over data collection, processing, and storage and hold companies accountable for mishandling personal information.

## ETHICAL USE IN SENSITIVE APPLICATIONS

Generative AI use in sensitive domains like healthcare or criminal justice poses unique risks. For example, in December 2024, CNN Health reported on the increasing use of AI chatbots for therapy, highlighting concerns from mental health experts about the accuracy and safety of the advice provided by these tools. Experts caution that while AI chatbots can offer immediate responses, they may lack the nuanced understanding required for effective mental health support, potentially leading to inappropriate or harmful guidance.

In criminal justice, imagine a generative AI model trained to draft police incident reports based on past data. While this might streamline administrative work, the AI could unintentionally incorporate biases in historical records, such as over-policing specific communities. This could result in fabricated narratives that unfairly target particular demographics, perpetuating systemic injustices.

To mitigate these risks in high-stakes contexts, generative AI must undergo extensive testing and validation. Collaboration with domain experts, such as medical professionals or legal scholars, supports alignment with ethical and professional standards.

## TRANSPARENCY AND ACCOUNTABILITY

Integrating generative AI into professional fields has brought significant ethical challenges, particularly in maintaining transparency and accountability. A recent example comes from the legal profession, where the New York City Bar Association, along with other state and national organizations, issued new ethical guidelines for lawyers' use of AI tools. These guidelines emphasize the importance of clear client communication, rigorous oversight of AI outputs, and adherence to professional standards.

Central to these guidelines is the "Seven C's" framework: Competence, Confidentiality, Consent, Confirmation, Conflicts, Candor, and Compliance. Each principle highlights a specific aspect of transparency and accountability necessary for responsibly deploying AI. For example:

- *Competence* requires lawyers to fully understand the generative AI tools they use, including their strengths and limitations.

- *Confidentiality* mandates that lawyers protect sensitive client data from being misused or exposed by AI tools, especially those operating on cloud-based platforms.
- *Consent* emphasizes the need to inform clients when AI tools are used for significant tasks, such as drafting contracts or analyzing case law.
- *Confirmation* underscores the lawyer's responsibility to verify AI-generated content.
- *Conflicts* address AI systems' potential to reuse client data, which could create ethical dilemmas.
- *Candor* obligates lawyers to promptly correct any errors or inaccuracies resulting from AI-generated outputs.
- *Compliance* requires adherence to court rules and ethical guidelines, ensuring AI's use aligns with legal standards and their clients' policies.

By establishing these principles, the legal profession proactively addresses the need for transparency and accountability in generative AI. Lawyers must disclose when and how AI tools are used and take responsibility for the outcomes they produce. Without these safeguards, client trust could be undermined, and the integrity of the legal process could be compromised.

## ACCESSIBILITY, EQUITY, INCLUSIVITY

In early 2024, in Davos, Switzerland, the AI Governance Alliance (AIGA)—an alliance that brings together business, government, and other experts—released three reports, the first of which focused on generative AI governance, and the second and third focusing on developing a framework for responsible development and deployment of AI, and unlocking its potential. About the AIGA, Cathy Li, Head of AI, Data and Metaverse at the World Economic Forum, stated:

> *The...Alliance is uniquely positioned to play a crucial role in furthering greater access to AI-related resources, thereby contributing to a more*

*equitable and responsible AI ecosystem globally.... We must collaborate among governments, the private sector and local communities to ensure the future of AI benefits all.*

Indeed, public-private partnerships like AIGA and others will be increasingly crucial to making AI accessible, inclusive, and equitable. This is important because it helps AI benefit everyone, reduces systemic biases rather than exacerbates them, promotes innovation, and supports ethical, culturally relevant, and sustainable solutions for diverse communities.

Generative AI offers immense potential to democratize access to technology, but its benefits remain unevenly distributed. Issues such as cost, infrastructure, language, and cultural relevance often exclude under-resourced regions and marginalized groups.

The financial and technical burden of advanced generative AI models is a significant barrier. OpenAI's newest models, for instance, generally require substantial computational power, making them accessible primarily to well-funded organizations in industrialized nations. Furthermore, these advanced systems often demand extensive infrastructure and technical expertise, widening the gap between resource-rich institutions and underfunded organizations.

Platforms like Hugging Face are critical in mitigating this issue. They provide open-source generative AI models, allowing smaller organizations and researchers to develop applications without prohibitive costs. These tools have become a lifeline for developers in underfunded institutions, enabling innovation in resource-constrained environments.

The World Bank's chatbot initiative, which utilizes generative AI to improve access to agricultural information, illustrates how global organizations can make these technologies more inclusive. This initiative provides farmers in developing nations with instant, AI-powered answers to questions about market prices, pest control, and irrigation techniques. Such chatbots reduce barriers to accessing critical knowledge, empowering rural communities with tools tailored to their needs.

In a more localized context, Farmerline's DARLI AI, a generative AI chatbot specifically designed for smallholder farmers in Ghana and other parts of Africa, demonstrates the importance of culturally and linguistically adapted solutions. By generating advice in local dialects and addressing region-specific farming challenges, DARLI AI bridges knowledge gaps in ways that global solutions may overlook. This hyper-localized approach ensures that farmers receive relevant, actionable guidance, highlighting how generative AI can be adapted to meet unique regional needs.

The challenge of linguistic inclusivity extends beyond regional efforts. Many generative AI systems are predominantly trained on English-language datasets, limiting their relevance for non-English speakers. Models like BLOOM, an open-source, multilingual AI, address this gap by supporting underrepresented languages. BLOOM's ability to generate text in over 50 languages demonstrates how inclusive design can expand the reach of generative AI.

Strategies like tiered pricing models, open-source frameworks, and culturally informed development practices are essential to guaranteeing that generative AI benefits everyone. By combining global initiatives with locally adapted solutions, the technology can evolve into a genuinely inclusive force, bridging divides and promoting innovation across diverse populations.

## NAVIGATING THE ETHICAL TIGHTROPE: SUPERALIGNMENT AND MISALIGNMENT IN AI

As generative AI systems become more sophisticated, ensuring they align with human values has become a critical ethical challenge. This challenge is encapsulated in a term that has recently gained traction: superalignment. Superalignment refers to the ability of generative AI systems to align their outputs and behavior with human values, ethical principles, and intended purposes. For example, a superaligned AI image generator consistently avoids producing harmful, misleading, or biased content, even in response to ambiguous prompts. Achieving superalignment requires robust training methods, diverse datasets, and continuous oversight to ensure systems remain adaptive to evolving ethical standards and cultural sensitivities.

Misalignment, by contrast, occurs when generative AI systems produce outputs that conflict with human expectations or ethical norms. This can result from biases in training data, poorly defined objectives, or unintended consequences of model behavior. For example, a misaligned AI text generator may unintentionally propagate stereotypes or create harmful misinformation, undermining trust in AI systems and causing real-world harm. These risks underscore the importance of addressing biases during development and implementing safeguards such as content moderation or human oversight to reduce the likelihood of ethical breaches.

A real-world example of potential misalignment is Meta's recent decision to scale back content moderation on its platforms, Facebook and Instagram. In January 2025, Meta CEO Mark Zuckerberg announced plans to eliminate third-party fact-checkers and replace them with a community-driven approach similar to X's Community Notes. While this shift is framed as an effort to promote free expression and reduce perceived bias, critics warn it is likely to increase misalignment between Meta's platform operations and societal values. Without robust professional oversight, the risk of misinformation, hate speech, and harmful content proliferating unchecked grows significantly, undermining both the quality of information available and user safety on these platforms.

In contrast, OpenAI's approach to superalignment initially appeared promising. In 2023, the company announced its superalignment team, tasked with mitigating risks associated with advanced AI models and improving user safety. This initiative reflected a commitment to ensuring ethical outcomes in AI. However, just one year later, the team was disbanded, and key figures such as co-founder Ilya Sutskever and Jan Leike departed the company, citing concerns over a perceived shift away from OpenAI's safety-first ethos. Their departures highlight the fragility of superalignment efforts and raise questions about whether even leading AI organizations can maintain their focus on long-term ethical commitments.

The tension between superalignment and misalignment underscores the broader ethical challenges of generative AI. The path forward will require collaboration among developers, policymakers, and stakeholders to create frameworks prioritizing transparency, accountability, and fairness. As users and stakeholders in a world increasingly shaped by AI, we all play a role in steering this technology toward ethical outcomes. By supporting transparent practices and holding organizations accountable, we can help make sure generative AI serves as a force for good.

* * *

## CHAPTER 8 SELF-ASSESSMENT

Reinforce your learning with a short and fun quiz. Just scan the QR code to get started. Alternatively, enter this URL into your browser: [**https://tinyurl.com/GenAI-Ch8-Quiz**].

QR code to access the Chapter 8 quiz.

# NINE
# VIGILANCE IN THE ERA OF GENERATIVE AI

Learning to distinguish AI-generated content is essential in a world where authenticity is increasingly scrutinized. This chapter demonstrates the importance of vigilance in a digital-first era and provides clear guidance on distinguishing real from fabricated.

## AI UNDER INVESTIGATION

Though generative AI creates incredibly lifelike images and videos, can clone voices with astonishing accuracy, and creates human-like text, it is still flawed, and there are, thankfully, ways to spot real from fake.

### AI-Generated Text

There are several things to look out for to help you spot AI-generated text, such as repetitive phrasing and over-perfection. Table 5 presents these and other aspects to consider when determining whether AI generated the text you're reading.

**Table 5: Recognizing AI-generated text**

| | |
|---|---|
| **Repetitive phrasing** | AI-generated text may overuse certain phrases or structures, leading to redundancy and a lack of variety in expression. |
| **Lack of personal insight** | AI-generated text often misses personal anecdotes or unique perspectives, resulting in a generic tone without specifics. |
| **Inconsistent contextual understanding** | AI may produce coherent text, but it is known to include statements that are completely made up, don't align with real-world facts, or don't align with common knowledge. This indicates AI's lack of true comprehension and underscores the importance of double-checking what you read. |
| **Over-perfection** | Content generated by AI tends to be grammatically flawless; it lacks the minor errors or colloquialisms that are typical in human writing. |
| **AI detection tools** | Utilize AI text detection tools like Scribbr's AI Content Detector to analyze and identify AI-generated text, offering detailed analysis at the paragraph level. Grammarly also provides AI detection tools. |

**A quick note on AI text detection tools:** While promising, these tools are far from perfect. In a personal experiment I conducted, I tested text that was 100% AI-generated alongside my writing. Maddeningly, the tool rated the AI-generated text more human-like than my writing! This example highlights the limitations of these tools and emphasizes the need for continued refinement in detecting AI-generated content. In another instance, I submitted *Essentials of AI Beginners* to a large distributor, and they initially rejected it, citing it was AI-generated. AI was responsible for detecting AI, and it didn't work so well, unfortunately compromising my ability to get my book into broader distribution. In the end, once a human looked at it instead of an AI, they saw that the writing was, in fact, my own. I am picking on AI-generated text detection tools only because I've had direct experience using them.

## AI-Generated Images and Cloned Voices

Thankfully, there are still ways to distinguish between real and AI-generated images and audio, as well as to identify cloned voices. While AI tools have become incredibly advanced, subtle differences still set human-created content apart from synthetic versions. Recognizing these distinctions is essential as AI-generated visuals and sounds become more prevalent across media, entertainment, and everyday communication.

To aid you in spotting AI-generated content, I invite you to review Tables 6 and 7, which outline key characteristics and detection techniques for AI-generated images and audio.

### Table 6: Spotting AI-generated images

| | |
|---|---|
| **Anatomical anomalies** | Pay attention to irregularities in human anatomy, such as:<br>• Distorted or asymmetrical facial features;<br>• Extra fingers;<br>• Unnatural limb proportions; and<br>• Feet where hands should be. |
| **Inconsistent lighting and shadows** | Look for lighting that doesn't align with the scene's context or shadows that fall in unnatural directions, as AI may struggle with consistent illumination. |
| **Texture irregularities** | Look for surfaces that appear overly smooth or lack the fine details present in real photographs, resulting in an unnatural look. |
| **AI detection tools** | Employ AI image detection tools like Illuminarty, which analyze images to determine if they were generated by AI, providing insights into their authenticity. |

### Table 7: Perceiving AI-generated audio and cloned voices

| | |
|---|---|
| **Unnatural speech patterns** | AI-generated text may overuse certain phrases or structures, leading to redundancy and a lack of variety in expression. |
| **Lack of emotional nuance** | Cloned voices often fail to capture the full range of human emotions, resulting in monotonous or overly uniform delivery. |
| **Background inconsistency** | AI-generated audio might lack ambient sounds or have inconsistent background noise, which can be a sign of synthetic production. |
| **Verification techniques** | In situations like unexpected calls requesting sensitive information, establish a "safe word" with family members to verify identities and prevent falling victim to voice cloning scams. |
| **AI detection tools** | Leverage tools such as Hiya's Deepfake Voice Detector or ElevenLabs AI Speech Classifier. Hiya's tool is a free browser extension and is more broadly applicable. In contrast, the ElevenLabs tool is meant to help users detect whether an audio clip was created using ElevenLabs voice cloning technology. |

## AI-Generated Videos

Here again, identifying AI-generated videos can be challenging, mainly due to the increasing sophistication of generative models. However, by paying close attention to specific details, you can spot inconsistencies that may indicate a video is AI-generated. Table 8 provides an overview of some key indicators.

### Table 8: Observing AI-generated videos

| | |
|---|---|
| **Facial irregularities** | Look out for:<br>• Unnatural eye movements: AI-generated videos may exhibit unnatural eye movements or inconsistent blinking patterns, which can make the subject appear less lifelike.<br>• Inconsistent lip syncing: There may be slight mismatches between the audio and the subject's lip movements, especially during rapid speech. |
| **Lighting and shadow discrepancies** | Pay attention to:<br>• Shadows that don't align correctly with the light source—this can indicate manipulation.<br>• Uneven skin tones: AI-generated videos might display skin tones that are too smooth or lack natural variation, resulting in an unnatural appearance. |
| **Background anomalies** | Distorted or static backgrounds: The background may appear warped or remain static while the subject moves, indicating possible AI generation. |
| **Unnatural movements** | Jerky or robotic motion: Subjects may exhibit movements that are not fluid, appearing mechanical or unnatural. |
| **Audio-visual mismatches** | Desynchronized audio: The audio may not perfectly sync with the visual elements, leading to a disjointed experience. |
| **Clothing and accessory artifacts** | Inconsistent accessories: Items like glasses or earrings may flicker, appear distorted, or not move naturally with the subject. |
| **Excessive perfection** | AI-generated subjects often lack imperfections such as pores or blemishes, resulting in an overly perfect look. |
| **Metadata analysis** | Review the video's metadata for inconsistencies or signs of tampering, which can indicate manipulation. |
| **Contextual verification** | Verify the video's content with reliable sources to ensure its authenticity. |

## THE IMPORTANCE OF VIGILANCE IN AN AI-DRIVEN ERA

Remember the good old days when the Milli Vanilli lip-syncing scandal shook the world? If you don't, that's probably because you weren't around—or were too young at the time to have felt the collective outrage. (Yes, I'm dating myself.) For those unfamiliar, Milli Vanilli was a pop duo that skyrocketed to fame in the late '80s, only to crash and burn when it was revealed they weren't singing on their tracks. It was a simpler time when "faking it" was considered scandalous and not a part of our everyday digital reality. Compared to today's AI-generated deepfakes, the Milli Vanilla scandal feels quaint. Now, the stakes are far higher, and instead of unmasking on-stage lip-syncers, we're left to determine whether the people we see on our screens are real.

"Two-faced." Image generated using DALL-E.

Unfortunately, no one is coming to save us from this challenge. The tools to detect AI-generated deception exist but are far from perfect; they are only as good as their training data and algorithms, leaving gaps in their ability to identify the most nuanced and sophisticated fakes. Furthermore, these detection tools can feel like a defensive arms race—always a step behind the next big breakthrough in generative AI technology. This means vigilance, critical thinking, and skepticism are essential survival tools in the modern age.

Determining what's real falls disproportionately on individuals, making education even more critical. Understanding the strengths and weaknesses of generative AI empowers you to approach suspicious content critically, much as we learned to spot red flags in phishing emails or identify questionable news sources during the rise of fake news. Sharing this knowledge within your circles—friends, family, and colleagues—amplifies its impact, creating a ripple effect of informed vigilance that strengthens community resilience.

Education alone is not enough. The sheer volume and quality of generative AI outputs can overwhelm even the most astute observers. This is why we must advocate for systemic solutions alongside personal responsibility. Media platforms, governments, and AI developers all have a role to play in implementing standards for authenticity and accountability. Whether through watermarking AI-generated content, labeling it transparently, or advancing detection technology, these systemic efforts can complement our individual vigilance.

## CHAPTER 9 SELF-ASSESSMENT

Are you ready for a recap? To access the end-of-chapter quiz, visit [**https://tinyurl.com/GenAI-Ch9-Quiz**] or scan the QR code to the right.

QR code to access the Chapter 9 quiz.

## BONUS ACTIVITY: CAN YOU SPOT REAL FROM FAKE?

Test your ability to distinguish real from fake. To access this bonus activity, scan the QR code to the right or visit the following URL: [**https://tinyurl.com/GenAI-RealvsFake**].

QR code to access the Real vs. Fake bonus activity.

# TEN
# AI IN ACTION: REAL-WORLD EXAMPLES

I enjoy sharing real-world examples of technology in action because they bring abstract concepts to life. We've already explored many examples of generative AI throughout this book; however, this chapter focuses on unique and lesser-known applications of the technology to demonstrate just how impactful generative AI can be.

As you read this chapter, consider how generative AI might be applied in your life or work. For instance, maybe you're interested in enhancing public services in your community, supporting a new business idea, improving your work processes, or sparking creativity in a hobby. Whatever your interest, let these examples inspire you.

## CULTURAL HERITAGE AND PRESERVATION

Generative and traditional AI work together to provide innovative ways to reconstruct, document, and engage with the past. Traditional AI primarily categorizes or catalogs historical data, while generative AI can create immersive experiences and digital restorations that bring history to life.

One significant application is digital restoration. Generative AI can analyze damaged artifacts, such as sculptures, paintings, or manuscripts, and reconstruct their missing parts based on historical records and artistic techniques. For instance, an AI model trained on similar works from the same era could digitally restore a partially destroyed fresco, recreating its original colors and details with remarkable accuracy.

Generative AI also transforms how people experience historical sites. By synthesizing data from archaeological findings, this technology can create virtual reconstructions of ancient cities, providing users with an unparalleled virtual reality experience. Just imagine yourself walking through a meticulously reconstructed Roman marketplace, complete with AI-generated sounds and visuals, or exploring an ancient Japanese temple from your living room. These immersive experiences make history accessible to wider audiences, from students to tourists, promoting a greater appreciation for cultural heritage.

## Digital restoration of the Dunhuang Murals

The Dunhuang murals in China's Mogao Caves are invaluable cultural artifacts dating back over a thousand years. Over time, exposure to environmental factors has led to their significant deterioration, including cracks, mold, and large-scale detachment.

Researchers developed a restoration method using generative adversarial networks,* or GANs, to digitally reconstruct damaged sections of the murals. The AI model was trained on high-resolution images of well-preserved mural sections to learn the intricate artistic styles and patterns. It then generated plausible restorations for the

---

* A GAN is an artificial intelligence framework consisting of two neural networks—a generator and a discriminator—that work together in a competitive process. The generator creates new data (such as images or text), while the discriminator evaluates the authenticity of the generated data against real data, improving the generator's output over time. GANs are widely used in creative applications like image restoration, art generation, and realistic simulations. For those interested, a more in-depth examination of GANs and how they work is included in *Essentials of AI for Beginners*.

damaged areas, filling in missing content while maintaining stylistic coherence.

The outcomes were impressive. The GAN-based approach produced restorations that closely aligned with the original artistic intent, preserving the murals' historical and aesthetic value. Furthermore, the digital restoration process significantly reduced the time and labor traditionally required for manual restoration, and the AI-generated restorations provide valuable digital records for future research and educational purposes.

### Virtual reconstruction of the Nameless Temple of Tipasa

The Nameless Temple of Tipasa is a UNESCO World Heritage Site in Algeria. Unfortunately, the temple has suffered extensive damage, leaving its original structure mainly to speculation.

Researchers employed text-to-image generative AI models to visually reconstruct the temple's access doors. How did they do this? They provided descriptive historical texts and archaeological data to the generative AI model, which, using these inputs, generated images of the temple's possible original appearance.

The outcomes of this research were three-fold: First, the AI-generated images provided archaeologists with visual hypotheses that guided further exploration and study. Second, the visual reconstructions enhanced the public's understanding of and appreciation for the site's historical significance. Lastly, the project informed conservation strategies by visualizing the temple's original state.

## DISASTER RESPONSE AND RECOVERY

Generative AI is modernizing our approaches to disaster management by enabling proactive planning and real-time responses. Traditional AI plays a key role in analyzing historical data, while generative AI enhances these efforts by creating dynamic strategies and communications that adapt to evolving crises, improving safety and resilience.

One transformative application is disaster scenario simulation.

While traditional AI and physical models simulate natural disasters like hurricanes or floods, generative AI can augment this by generating alternative preparedness strategies, such as proposing multiple evacuation routes, generating resource distribution plans, or developing contingency scenarios based on the simulated impact of a hurricane on a coastal city.

Generative AI enhances real-time communication during emergencies by crafting multilingual and region-specific alerts tailored to affected populations. Additionally, it can analyze live data from sensors, drones, and social media to provide emergency teams with updated response strategies, aiding in adaptive and effective disaster management.

### FloodBrain's flood disaster reporting

Rapid and accurate disaster impact reporting is crucial for providing practical humanitarian assistance. Traditional methods often face challenges in swiftly processing vast amounts of data, which can delay response efforts.

This is where FloodBrain comes into play. Researchers developed this tool that employs LLMs to generate comprehensive flood disaster impact reports. The system integrates real-time web data to produce detailed and accurate assessments of flood events. The key features of FloodBrain include web-based data integration, report generation, and comparison with human reports. Floodbrain aggregates information from various online sources to keep reports current and comprehensive. Utilizing LLMs, the tool crafts coherent narratives that detail the extent and impact of flooding, aiding in situational awareness. Finally, evaluations of FloodBrain's AI-generated reports are comparable in quality to those produced by human experts, with the added advantage of rapid production.

Deploying FloodBrain leads to crucial outcomes, including quickly generating detailed reports to enable faster decision-making and resource allocation during flood emergencies. This tool can also handle large volumes of data and is adaptable to disaster scenarios beyond flooding.

## ENERGY AND ENVIRONMENT

Generative AI is increasingly being explored to tackle challenges in the energy and environmental sectors, complementing the foundational work of traditional AI. While traditional AI excels in analyzing historical data and making predictions, generative AI creates innovative designs and actionable solutions that align with sustainability goals. For example, generative AI is used in urban planning to design eco-friendly structures and green spaces that harmonize with natural ecosystems.

### Automating urban park design with GANs

A study conducted by researchers at Beijing Forestry University employed GANs to automate the design of urban parks. The AI model generated park layouts that effectively integrated various design elements, demonstrating the potential of generative AI in creating well-organized and innovative green spaces. This approach allows for the rapid exploration of design alternatives, ensuring that urban development aligns with ecological preservation and community well-being.

### Floating solar panel design in Japan

Japan faces significant land constraints, making large-scale solar installations challenging. To address this, the country has turned to floating solar farms on reservoirs and lakes. Industrial designer Satoshi Yanagisawa collaborated with a Japanese renewable energy company to design an innovative float mechanism for water-based solar power generation. Utilizing generative design software, they input various constraints and performance criteria, allowing the AI to explore numerous design permutations. This process led to creating an optimized float structure that effectively supports solar panels while withstanding water currents and weather conditions, and minimizes material usage, resulting in cost savings and reduced environmental impact, as well as significantly shortening development timelines.

## HOUSING AND HOMELESSNESS

When researching examples of generative AI in action for this book, I never thought AI could help solve housing and homelessness challenges, yet here we are! The unhoused population in large US cities can be staggeringly high, with New York City and Los Angeles topping the list with more than 88,000 and 71,000 people, respectively, in need of affordable, accessible, and safe shelter. Generative AI could be deployed to reimagine shelter solutions with modular, portable housing designs tailored to specific needs, offering those who need these shelters the dignity they deserve and the opportunity to improve their lives. Generative AI can optimize layouts so that each structure maximizes space and comfort while maintaining ease of transport and assembly.

### Solutions for housing and homelessness in California

In 2023, Governor Gavin Newsom announced an initiative to explore how generative AI can address critical social challenges, including housing affordability and homelessness, through innovative technological solutions. The initiative seeks to capitalize on California's status as a global technology leader to enhance resource allocation for vulnerable populations.

One key goal is developing an AI-powered platform that provides real-time updates on available shelter and treatment beds for unhoused individuals. The platform would integrate data from local jurisdictions, shelters, and healthcare facilities to deliver accurate, timely resource information. It would feature tailored user interfaces, including region-specific dashboards and mobile-friendly access for local governments and service providers. Such a tool could significantly improve service efficiency by helping caseworkers quickly match individuals to the nearest available beds and support services, reducing delays in aid distribution.

California also aims to apply AI in streamlining housing development and policymaking. Generative AI can analyze permitting data to clarify complex local approvals, improving transparency and efficiency in the development process. Additionally, AI can identify gaps in housing supply, such as areas with low construction rates, and generate actionable insights for policymakers. Furthermore, it can propose innovative, community-specific housing designs that optimize land use while aligning with local needs. By harnessing generative AI's ability to analyze and present complex data, California seeks to accelerate housing construction and expand access for vulnerable populations.

## HUMANITARIAN AID: SUPPORT FOR REFUGEES

Crowded refugee camps are, tragically, all too common. According to the International Rescue Committee (IRC), in 2024, more than 117 million people were forced from their homes, many winding up in refugee camps. In these places, optimism seems distant, but the deployment of generative AI could offer a beacon of hope. For example, generative AI can craft multilingual educational materials that bridge language barriers, providing displaced communities access to vital information and learning opportunities. This technology can also translate complex legal documents into understandable guides, empowering refugees to navigate the legal landscapes of their new homes. Real-world initiatives, such as partnerships between humanitarian organizations and AI developers, are already demonstrating the power of AI to deliver critical resources efficiently and equitably.

### AI-powered chatbots for refugee assistance

The IRC has implemented AI-driven chatbots to support refugees by providing real-time, multilingual information on critical topics such as asylum procedures, healthcare services, and education opportunities. These chatbots apply generative AI to deliver accurate and contextually relevant responses, thereby enhancing the accessibility of vital information for displaced populations.

The IRC's Signpost Project utilizes AI to disseminate crucial information to displaced individuals, aiding them in locating safety and services while countering misinformation. By 2024, the Signpost Project had reached over 18 million people across 17 countries, providing essential information in multiple languages and significantly improving the efficiency of humanitarian responses.

**Education in crisis-affected regions**

Projects like AprendAI, Lelapa AI, and OpenAI's educational initiatives are advancing AI-driven solutions to enhance and personalize education for children affected by crises, with a strong emphasis on local language content to maintain relevance and accessibility.

AprendAI, developed by the International Rescue Committee (IRC) in partnership with OpenAI, is an AI-powered educational chatbot platform designed to support teachers and caregivers in crisis-affected communities. It aims to rapidly deploy personalized learning experiences via widely used messaging platforms, with an initial goal of reaching 10,000 teachers and caregivers across regions such as Northeast Nigeria, Colombia, and Bangladesh—ultimately impacting over half a million students.

Lelapa AI, a Johannesburg-based startup, focuses on AI solutions for African languages. Its flagship product, Vulavula, facilitates transcription, conversation analysis, translation, and speech synthesis in languages such as isiZulu, Sesotho, Afrikaans, and English. By expanding AI capabilities in underserved linguistic communities, Lelapa AI is making AI-driven education more inclusive.

OpenAI has also partnered with Common Sense Media to launch a free AI training course for teachers. This initiative demystifies artificial intelligence and prompt engineering, equipping educators with the tools to integrate AI responsibly into their teaching.

These initiatives, which utilize generative AI to overcome

language and accessibility barriers, have the potential to provide quality education to thousands of children with limited access to traditional learning resources, empowering them with growth opportunities even in the most challenging circumstances.

## LICENSING AND REGULATION

Regulatory bodies are essential for ensuring that professionals in healthcare, engineering, law, and accounting uphold the highest standards of competence and accountability. Regulatory bodies face increasing demands to manage complex workflows, oversee continuing education, investigate unethical practices, and resolve complaints fairly and efficiently. Generative AI can transform how regulatory bodies meet these challenges, enabling them to streamline processes, enhance transparency, and uphold fairness in their oversight roles.

### The Federation of State Medical Boards' ethical guidelines for AI integration in healthcare

The Federation of State Medical Boards (FSMB), a nonprofit organization representing medical boards across the United States, offers an excellent, real-world example demonstrating how generative AI is modernizing professional regulation and shaping ethical practices in healthcare.

FSMB has long been a leader in developing policies safeguarding public safety in medical practice. In 2024, the FSMB released its landmark policy document, "Navigating the Responsible and Ethical Incorporation of Artificial Intelligence into Clinical Practice," which provides a comprehensive framework for integrating AI tools, including generative AI, into healthcare settings.

While AI tools are widely used for predictive analytics in healthcare, the FSMB's guidelines highlight the growing potential of generative AI to create innovative, patient-centered solutions. One notable application is using generative AI to develop personalized treatment simulations and training scenarios that reflect real-world complexities. For instance, generative tools can model ethical dilemmas, such as allocating limited resources, addressing diverse patient needs, and offering clinicians nuanced, practice-based learning opportunities.

The FSMB framework emphasizes the importance of education, accountability, and transparency in using generative AI. Key principles include:

- *Beneficence:* Ensuring AI applications prioritize patient well-being and improve outcomes.
- *Non-Maleficence:* Avoiding harm by setting clear boundaries on using AI in clinical decision-making.
- *Justice:* Promoting equitable access to AI benefits while addressing potential biases in AI systems.
- *Autonomy:* Respecting patients' right to informed consent when using generative AI tools in their care.

The FSMB also stresses that clinicians—not AI—must remain ultimately responsible for medical decisions; AI serves as a tool to enhance, not replace, professional judgment. Additionally, the guidelines address critical issues such as liability, data privacy, and the importance of building trust in AI applications.

The policy's impact is significant. It empowers state medical boards to responsibly oversee the integration of AI into healthcare, helping to keep ethical standards and public safety at the forefront. By providing actionable recommendations, the framework helps medical boards navigate emerging challenges, such as liability concerns and transparency, while encouraging innovation.

This policy bridges the gap between technological advancements and ethical practice, offering a roadmap for how generative AI can enhance healthcare delivery without compromising professional and ethical standards. It is a model for other regulatory bodies looking to adopt AI responsibly in their respective fields.

## NONPROFIT AND SOCIAL GOOD ORGANIZATIONS

Generative AI is reshaping how nonprofits and social good organizations operate, enabling them to maximize their impact with limited resources. By producing tailored content and outreach strategies, generative AI allows these organizations to connect deeply with their audiences, amplifying their message and mission.

Campaign creation is one of the most transformative uses of generative AI in this sector. Nonprofits often rely on emotionally compelling visuals and narratives to rally support for causes, but traditional approaches can take weeks or months to create. With generative AI, organizations can design visually impactful materials and craft messaging tailored to specific demographics within hours. For example, an organization raising awareness about child hunger can use generative AI to produce infographics, videos, and social media posts that resonate with different audiences. AI analyzes data from past campaigns, audience preferences, and current trends to generate content that aligns perfectly with the organization's goals.

Another crucial application is in educational outreach, especially in underserved regions. Generative AI can create custom learning materials tailored to local contexts, adapting language and visuals to address cultural and literacy differences. Imagine an AI tool generating interactive textbooks in multiple dialects or creating animated lessons that explain health and hygiene concepts to children in remote communities! This technology bridges the educational divide, ensuring that marginalized populations gain access to vital knowledge and skills.

### Opportunity International's AI initiatives

The nonprofit organization Opportunity International has developed a generative AI chatbot, Ulangizi, to provide agricultural advice to farmers in rural Malawi. This chatbot delivers personalized guidance in the local language, Chichewa, helping farmers improve their practices and productivity. Opportunity International has also funded AI-driven applications to assist teachers in lesson planning and support school leaders with administrative tasks, aiming to democratize education and agricultural knowledge in high-poverty areas.

**Enuma's AI-enabled educational tools**

Enuma develops educational applications that utilize generative AI, including language learning models, to support children in underserved communities. Their products are designed to function in multiple native languages, such as Swahili, Malay, English, and Korean, making them accessible to a diverse user base. By collaborating with global organizations, including the United Nations, Enuma has delivered AI-enabled education to Rohingya refugee children, addressing their specific language needs and promoting inclusive learning.

* * *

## CHAPTER 10 SELF-ASSESSMENT

End this chapter on a high note by testing your knowledge and recollection with this end-of-chapter quiz. Simply scan the QR code below to the right, or visit this link: [**https://tinyurl.com/GenAI-Ch10-Quiz**].

QR code to access the Chapter 10 Quiz.

# ELEVEN
# LEARNING BY DOING: PRACTICAL AND INTERACTIVE ACTIVITIES

> Tell me and I forget, teach me and I remember, involve me and I learn."
>
> BENJAMIN FRANKLIN, FOUNDING FATHER OF THE UNITED STATES, SCIENTIST, AND INVENTOR

Interactive learning has long been recognized as one of the most effective ways to grasp new concepts, develop skills, and spark creativity. With the advent of generative AI, interactive learning is entering an entirely new phase—one where learners can actively engage with AI-driven tools to personalize their experience, collaborate in unique ways, and solve real-world challenges. Whether you're a student, a professional, or a curious mind looking to explore, generative AI empowers you to go beyond passive consumption and actively participate in the learning process.

In this chapter, I'll introduce you to two practical hands-on activities. Step-by-step instructions are available as digital, downloadable resources accessible via QR codes and intuitive links. The activities outlined in this chapter are designed to demonstrate the potential of generative AI and equip you with the skills to use it effectively in your personal, professional, and entrepreneurial pursuits. By the end, you'll see how AI can turn learning into a dynamic and creative journey tailored just for you.

## HANDS-ON EXERCISES FOR ACTIVE ENGAGEMENT

### Activity 1: Creating Custom Courses with ChatGPT Using the Prompt Chaining Technique

Developing a tailored educational program from scratch typically involves collaboration among various professionals, each contributing specific expertise to create a comprehensive and engaging learning experience. Typical roles involved in such an undertaking include subject matter experts, instructional designers, graphic designers and multimedia specialists, e-learning developers, content editors, project managers, quality assurance specialists, and more. Furthermore, creating a custom course in the traditional way can take months or even longer. Now, I am not advocating for doing away with traditional approaches to course development, but my goal is to show you another way, using generative AI. You see, with this technology, you can create the content for a custom course yourself in a matter of hours. This activity works well in many scenarios, including these:

- *Entrepreneurs monetizing knowledge:* Use this method to create and sell courses, turning your expertise into a lucrative revenue stream.
- *Educators enhancing class materials:* Create custom lessons or units for classroom use, adapting to the specific needs of your students or curriculum.
- *Corporate training programs:* Design onboarding programs, compliance training, or skill development modules tailored to your organization's requirements.

- *Nonprofits and community education:* Develop free or low-cost courses for underserved populations, focusing on skills like financial literacy or career readiness.
- *Content creators building a brand:* Add value to your audience by offering exclusive courses, enhancing engagement, and building credibility.

These are only a few cases where this activity could be beneficial. As you work through this activity, I invite you to consider how this could benefit your life and work.

This activity will teach you how to use prompt chaining to design a complete course systematically. By starting with clear goals and refining the AI's output at each step, you will create a polished course that is personalized for your audience and ready for implementation.

QR code to access the tutorial for Activity 1: Creating Custom Courses.

To get started, scan the QR code to the right or visit [**tinyurl.com/GenAI-Activity-1**].

## Activity 2: Building a Generative Pre-Trained Transformer (GPT)

Creating a custom generative pre-trained transformer (GPT) may sound like an undertaking reserved for tech giants or AI experts. Traditionally, building an AI model requires a team of professionals, including data scientists, machine learning engineers, software developers, and project managers. This process involves gathering and curating vast datasets, writing complex algorithms, and allocating substantial computational resources. For businesses or individuals without access to such expertise or funding, this would typically be out of reach. However, thanks to advancements in generative AI platforms, creating your own custom GPT has become accessible, affordable, and surprisingly simple.

Now, let me be clear: this activity isn't about replacing the depth of custom-built models developed by major corporations or research institutions. Instead, the goal is to empower you to create an AI assistant tailored to your needs—whether for personal projects, small businesses, or nonprofit ventures. With tools like CustomGPT.ai, you can bypass much of the technical complexity and focus on shaping an AI tool that aligns perfectly with your goals, using your own data sources and preferences.

You may remember me introducing you to "Aiden," the AI-driven personal assistant introduced in the book's introduction. Aiden was designed to be a tireless colleague—writing emails, summarizing reports, designing presentations, brainstorming ideas, and more. In this activity, you'll take a hands-on approach to creating your own real-world "Aiden," a GPT uniquely equipped to meet your specific needs. If you're building an AI assistant for your business, personal productivity, or a community project, this is your opportunity to bring your vision to life. This activity is incredibly versatile, offering value in a wide range of scenarios:

- *Entrepreneurs streamlining operations:* Use a custom GPT to handle customer inquiries, automate scheduling, or provide product recommendations.
- *Nonprofits improving outreach:* Create a GPT that answers FAQs about your services, freeing up staff for more impactful work.
- *Educators enhancing accessibility:* Design a virtual tutor for students, answering questions and reinforcing learning in specific subject areas.
- *Corporate teams boosting productivity:* Build a knowledge assistant for internal use, helping employees find relevant policies, documents, or training materials quickly.
- *Content creators engaging audiences:* Develop a GPT that interacts with your followers, sharing insights or answering common questions in your unique voice.

These are just a few ways this activity can add value to your work and life. Think about the specific tasks or challenges you face —as chances are, a custom GPT could simplify them.

In this activity, you'll learn to build a personalized GPT step by step using an accessible, no-code platform. You'll define the model's purpose, upload knowledge sources, customize its tone and behavior, and test its output—all without needing any technical expertise. The result? A powerful AI tool that reflects your goals, values, and unique context—your very own "Aiden" ready to assist, create, and innovate on your behalf.

QR code to access the tutorial for Activity 2: Building a Custom GPT.

The tutorial for this activity can be accessed via the QR code to the right or this URL: [**tinyurl.com/GenAI-Activity-2**].

* * *

## CHAPTER 11 SELF-ASSESSMENT

Reinforce what you've learned by taking the end-of-chapter quiz. Scan the QR code to the right, or enter the following URL into your browser: [**https://tinyurl.com/GenAI-Ch11-Quiz**].

QR code to access the Chapter 11 quiz.

# TWELVE
# GENERATIVE AI IN FLUX: LAW, BUSINESS, AND THE SHIFTING SOCIAL CONTRACT

## AI AND THE SOCIAL CONTRACT: A NEW DEAL FOR SOCIETY

Generative AI is currently and will continue to challenge legal and regulatory frameworks, redefine corporate strategies, and reshape economies. However, this technology also challenges the current social contract—the unspoken agreement between people and their society about how we live together—what rights we have, what duties we accept, and what the government is responsible for. With AI, this unspoken agreement is beginning to change. For example, traditionally, the social contract of work has been based on a simple understanding: If you get an education, develop skills, and work hard, you will have stable employment and financial security. In return, companies provide wages, benefits, and growth opportunities. Governments also regulate labor laws, ensure fair pay, and provide social safety nets. But, in this age of artificial intelligence, the social contract of work we enjoy is changing profoundly. Let's examine three key ways AI is reshaping the social contract of work.

***Automation versus job security.*** AI and automation are replacing jobs (e.g., factory work, customer service, legal document review), making the old promise of stable employment less certain. Workers must continually reskill rather than rely on a lifelong career in one field.

***Gig work and algorithmic management.*** Many jobs are shifting from full-time to gig work (e.g., Uber, DoorDash, Upwork, and other freelance platforms). AI-driven algorithms determine work assignments, wages, and who gets blocked or deactivated from a platform. This changes the traditional worker-employer relationship—people now often work for an AI rather than a human boss.

***New ethical and regulatory questions.*** Governments are struggling to update policies to protect workers in an AI-driven economy. Should there be universal basic income (UBI) if AI takes over too many jobs? Who is responsible if an AI system unfairly denies someone a job or promotion?

The traditional understanding of work—"I provide labor, and in return, I get stability and fair treatment"—is being disrupted, with AI playing an increasingly significant role. Now, workers must navigate AI-driven decisions, continuous learning, and the decline of traditional job security, leading to calls for new regulations, ethical AI, and social safety nets.

But the current social contract isn't only about work. It also underpins democratic governance, laws, and civil rights and serves as the basis for addressing societal challenges like inequality, public health, education, and social justice. I am bringing awareness to this because technologies like generative AI do challenge labor markets (as all new technologies inevitably do), but they also challenge privacy (balancing individual data rights and societal benefits from data-driven innovation) and accountability. Many scholars and AI experts argue that technologies like generative AI could necessitate a revision of the social contract to uphold fairness, ethical use, and shared prosperity in our increasingly AI-driven world. Is this concerning? Yes, I think so. Thankfully, good work is being done to address how AI is challenging the social contract. The following organizations and initiatives provide a few excellent examples.

- *AI for Good Initiative.* Spearheaded by the International Telecommunications Union (ITU) in partnership with the United Nations, this initiative focuses on using AI to tackle global challenges such as poverty, health, and climate change.
- *The Algorithmic Justice League (AJA)* works to highlight and combat bias in AI systems. It advocates for transparency and fairness in AI development. Dr. Joy Buolamwini, the bestselling author of *Unmasking AI: My Mission to Protect What is Human in a World of Machines*, founded AJA.
- *The Berkman Klein Center for Internet and Society at Harvard University* works on many projects aimed at algorithms and justice, artificial intelligence and the law, responsible generative AI, and more.
- *Global Partnership on Artificial Intelligence (GPAI)* is an international initiative supported by over 25 member states, including Canada, the UK, and India. GPAI conducts multi-disciplinary research on AI's societal impacts, promotes international cooperation on ethical AI standards and data governance, and funds projects focused on inclusive AI, which includes tools for low-income and marginalized communities.

These efforts underscore the growing recognition that generative AI must be aligned with societal values to prevent harm while promoting innovation.

## DATA USE AND LEGAL DISPUTES

Multiple legal challenges have targeted OpenAI in India. A coalition of Indian and international book publishers—including Bloomsbury, Penguin Random House, and Cambridge University

Press—filed a lawsuit in New Delhi, alleging that OpenAI's ChatGPT accesses proprietary content without proper licensing. Similarly, major Indian digital news firms, including those owned by billionaires Gautam Adani and Mukesh Ambani, have accused OpenAI of using copyrighted news content without permission.

In a separate case, OpenAI has requested an Indian court to dismiss a lawsuit filed by a group of Indian and global book publishers accusing it of copyright violations. The publishers argue that ChatGPT generates book summaries and extracts from unlicensed copies, harming their business. OpenAI counters that its platform only uses publicly available data sourced from websites like Wikipedia or from summaries made available by the publishers themselves.

Beyond OpenAI, other tech companies are facing similar scrutiny. LinkedIn is currently contending with a class-action lawsuit in California, accused of using private messages from its premium users to train AI models without explicit consent. The lawsuit alleges that LinkedIn altered its privacy settings to opt users into AI training without their knowledge.

In Canada, several media companies, including The Globe and Mail, have filed a lawsuit against OpenAI, alleging that its models have been trained on copyrighted Canadian news content without proper licensing. The plaintiffs argue that AI-generated summaries and repurposed articles negatively impact their revenue streams and undermine original journalism. This lawsuit marks a significant development in the global legal landscape surrounding AI and intellectual property.

These cases highlight the challenges of balancing AI-driven innovation with intellectual property rights. As lawsuits multiply, it becomes increasingly clear that regulatory clarity is needed to define how AI models can source and utilize data responsibly.

## REGULATORY SCRUTINY AND MARKET FAIRNESS

Globally, governments are grappling with how to regulate AI in ways that promote innovation, fair competition, and prevent monopolistic dominance. However, regulatory approaches vary widely, reflecting different economic and political priorities.

In the United States, the regulatory landscape has shifted significantly with the change in administration. Former President Biden's Executive Order 14110, issued on October 30, 2023, sought to establish comprehensive guidelines for the safe and trustworthy development of AI. However, this order was rescinded by President Trump upon assuming office on January 20, 2025, signaling a shift toward minimal regulatory intervention aimed at accelerating AI development. While this approach prioritizes rapid AI advancement, it has also raised concerns about monopolistic practices and the need for balanced oversight.

While the U.S. moves toward deregulation, other global powers are taking markedly different approaches. China has implemented national AI regulations requiring annual social responsibility reports and defining "negative lists" for high-risk AI research, which are restricted categories of AI development that are deemed to pose significant ethical, security, or societal risks. These measures aim to guarantee that AI development aligns with societal values and ethical standards.

In the European Union, the recently enacted EU AI Act establishes one of the world's most comprehensive legal frameworks for artificial intelligence. It categorizes AI applications into unacceptable, high, and minimal or no risk levels and imposes corresponding regulatory requirements. For instance, AI systems deemed high-risk, such as those used in critical infrastructure or education, are subject to strict obligations to ensure safety and protect fundamental rights.

Together, these examples illustrate the diverse regulatory strategies shaping AI's future. With AI's global reach, how these differing approaches will unfold in practice remains to be seen.

This diversity in regulatory approaches highlights the

complexity of crafting effective AI governance. As Clément (Clem) Delangue, the co-founder and CEO of Hugging Face, an open and collaborative platform for AI builders, noted during the House hearing on AI—Advancing Innovation in the National Interest (June 24, 2023), AI's broad impact means that regulation cannot take a one-size-fits-all approach. He emphasized that regulation should be *"customized and focused on specific domains, use cases, and sectors where there are more risks,"* allowing the broader AI ecosystem to continue growing and innovating.

This perspective underscores regulators' challenge: balancing oversight with promoting innovation while addressing AI's global and cross-industry implications. The effectiveness of these varied approaches will ultimately depend on how well they navigate these competing priorities.

## CORPORATE STRATEGIES IN AI EXPANSION

As generative AI reshapes industries, corporations increasingly integrate AI into their strategies to improve efficiency and maintain their competitive advantage. However, as AI adoption accelerates, concerns about regulatory compliance, ethical considerations, and monopolistic behavior have also intensified.

OpenAI, for instance, aims to serve a billion users through partnerships with Apple and other major firms, underscoring its ambition to dominate the AI landscape. Meanwhile, Amazon's $8 billion investment in Anthropic highlights the race among tech giants to secure leadership in AI development. These massive investments signal AI's growing role in shaping digital infrastructure and consumer experiences.

However, these aggressive AI expansion strategies have drawn regulatory attention. The U.S. Federal Trade Commission (FTC) has begun scrutinizing AI partnerships for potential antitrust violations. Similar investigations are underway in the EU, where regulators examine whether tech giants' AI alliances could stifle competition and reinforce existing monopolies.

Beyond big tech, AI-driven automation is transforming traditional sectors. In the financial industry, the Commonwealth Bank of Australia has incorporated AI-powered chatbots to improve customer service, while legal firms in Australia and New Zealand use generative AI to automate contract analysis so lawyers can focus on higher-value work. These applications demonstrate how AI is streamlining operations, though they also prompt ethical concerns about workforce displacement and data privacy.

## INFLECTION POINT

Generative AI is at an inflection point. The rapid evolution of its legal, regulatory, and corporate landscapes underscores the complexities of integrating this technology into society. As intellectual property disputes continue, governments refine AI policies, and corporations push for dominance, the stakes for ethical and responsible AI development have never been higher. Whether through proactive regulation, corporate accountability, or international cooperation, ensuring that AI benefits all of society—not just a select few—will be one of the defining challenges of the coming years.

* * *

## CHAPTER 12 SELF-ASSESSMENT

Wrap up this chapter by scanning the following QR to take a short quiz. Alternatively, visit this link to test your knowledge: [**https://tinyurl.com/GenAI-Ch12-Quiz**].

QR code to access the Chapter 12 quiz.

# THIRTEEN
# THE ROAD AHEAD: WHERE GENERATIVE AI IS HEADED NEXT

AI is evolving at a dizzying pace, blurring the lines between what we once imagined and what is now possible. While the future of AI—especially generative AI—remains somewhat unpredictable, analyzing today's breakthroughs can offer a glimpse into what's next.

## ALL THE RAGE: AGENTIC AI AND AUTONOMOUS AGENTS

Agentic AI is reshaping artificial intelligence by enabling systems to make decisions, execute tasks, and manage workflows with minimal human oversight. Unlike traditional AI, which requires explicit instructions, these systems exhibit self-sufficiency, adapting dynamically to new information and generating real-time solutions.

OpenAI's Operator, launched as a research preview in January 2025, represents a major step forward. Operator can autonomously navigate websites and complete transactions to book tickets, order groceries, and manage appointments. While still in early development, it showcases AI's growing integration into daily life.

Businesses harness agentic AI to optimize supply chains, automate customer support, and analyze financial data. Marketing teams use AI agents to create personalized campaigns, while HR departments rely on them for recruitment and candidate screening. For individuals, AI-powered financial assistants automate budgeting, while shopping agents compare prices and place orders based on user preferences.

The rise of agentic AI may require reexamining societal structures as automation encroaches on jobs once considered safe from disruption. If trends continue, discussions around universal basic income and AI-taxed revenue redistribution will become more pressing. Ethical concerns also persist, particularly around transparency and accountability. Explainable AI (XAI) aims to make these systems more interpretable so their decisions can be audited and understood.

Beyond OpenAI's Operator, notable developments include AutoGPT, BabyAGI, and DeepMind's adaptive AI models, which refine strategies independently. Microsoft's AI-driven workflow automation enables enterprises to develop self-improving AI agents that enhance business efficiency. Elon Musk's xAI has also introduced Grok-3, an advanced AI model leveraging ten times the computing power of its predecessor. Grok-3 is designed to compete with leading AI systems like GPT-4 and DeepSeek V3, claiming superior performance in mathematics, science, and coding. This latest advancement highlights the fast-paced evolution of autonomous AI agents capable of refining strategies and optimizing workflows. Agentic AI can revolutionize governance, urban planning, and emergency response management; however, responsible deployment remains critical. Balancing automation with ethical oversight to maximize innovation while mitigating risks is imperative.

## THE CONTINUED RISE OF MULTIMODAL AI

Multimodal AI is gaining traction as models evolve to process multiple forms of data for more human-like perception and interaction. Industry analysts predict a significant increase in AI systems integrating multiple modalities in the years ahead.

While some models combine text and images, others incorporate real-time audio and video inputs, leading to more dynamic applications. For example, Netflix is refining its recommendation engine by analyzing viewing histories alongside textual and audio cues. At the same time, Walmart employs AI-driven inventory management that merges camera feeds, sales data, and shelf availability insights.

In healthcare, multimodal AI integrates medical imaging, patient histories, and real-time sensor data from wearables to aid diagnostics and treatment planning. In education, virtual tutors use speech, video, and text to deliver personalized learning experiences.

Regulatory compliance, high computing costs, and data privacy remain concerns, and ethical issues such as deepfakes and AI-generated misinformation must also be addressed. Despite these hurdles, multimodal AI promises to redefine digital experiences, from connected home ecosystems to AI-powered customer service bots.

## AI-DRIVEN SCIENCE AND MEDICINE

Generative AI is accelerating breakthroughs in medicine and drug discovery. For example, Manas AI, co-founded by Reid Hoffman and Dr. Siddhartha Mukherjee, applies AI-driven computational chemistry to identify promising therapeutic candidates. Partnering with Microsoft Azure, the company conducts molecular docking simulations at speeds dramatically surpassing traditional methods.

MIT's FrameDiff tool and DeepMind's AlphaFold and ProteinMPNN are revolutionizing protein design, generating unique structures that could advance gene therapy and disease treatment. Also, companies like Insilico Medicine use AI to propose new molecular candidates, accelerating the research of oncology and antiviral therapies. Insilico Medicine employs generative AI to design novel molecular structures for various diseases, leveraging deep learning and GANs to identify potential drug candidates. The company has advanced a preclinical candidate for idiopathic pulmonary fibrosis into human clinical trials, marking a significant milestone in AI-driven drug development.

A notable recent entrant in this field is Latent Labs, a biotech startup founded by former DeepMind scientist Simon Kohl. Backed by $50 million in funding, Latent Labs collaborates with pharmaceutical firms to design synthetic proteins that could form the basis of new antibody treatments. By leveraging generative AI, the company seeks to replace some traditional experimental methods with computational approaches, significantly reducing the time and cost of drug development. This innovation could open doors to entirely new classes of medicines designed by AI from the ground up.

AI is poised to profoundly redefine medical research, diagnostics, and treatment development. Unsurprisingly, regulatory approval remains a hurdle: rigorous validation is required before AI-generated drugs can be released into the market.

## PERSONALIZED AI: WEARABLES AND PERSONAL ASSISTANTS

AI-powered wearables are evolving from basic fitness trackers to intelligent personal assistants that offer dynamic, predictive, and adaptive support.

The Humane AI Pin projects AI-generated content onto surfaces, while the Rabbit R1, launched in late 2024, provides hands-free assistance by learning user preferences and integrating with smart home devices. In healthcare, Whoop's AI-driven coach delivers personalized fitness recommendations, while Fitbit users can integrate third-party AI apps for custom training plans.

Beyond fitness, AI-powered wearables like Friend act as social companions, offering conversational interactions and tailored suggestions. Emerging solutions include real-time language translation, personal safety features, and home security integrations.

While promising, AI wearables face some adoption challenges due to cost, battery life, and privacy concerns. Transparency in data practices and accessibility improvements will be key to mainstream adoption.

## INTEGRATION WITH AR/VR AND IMMERSIVE EXPERIENCES

Augmented reality (AR) and virtual reality (VR) are improving thanks to generative AI that creates deeply interactive, personalized environments.

"Woman wearing augmented reality glasses in a foggy cyberpunk setting." Generated using Freepik, Flux 1.0 model.

OpenAI's Sora model, for instance, generates hyper-realistic video content, paving the way for more immersive AR/VR experiences. Another example is Meta's Codec Avatars, which enhance digital interactions, while NVIDIA's Omniverse enables the creation of photorealistic AI-generated worlds.

In education, AI-driven VR simulations immerse students in historical events or scientific concepts. In healthcare, AI-powered VR therapy treats PTSD, phobias, and anxiety disorders. Furthermore, surgical training simulations offer lifelike practice environments for medical professionals.

Hardware limitations, cost barriers, and psychological impacts, such as over-immersion risks, must be addressed. However, as AI-generated environments become more sophisticated, they will affect how we learn, heal, and interact with technology.

## GENERATIVE AI IN SEARCH: A NEW ERA FOR INFORMATION RETRIEVAL

Traditional search engines rely on keyword-based indexing, often requiring users to sift through multiple sources to find the answers they seek. Generative AI is changing this by providing context-aware summaries rather than just lists of links.

Companies like Google, Microsoft, and Apple are integrating AI-generated summaries, conversational search interfaces, and personalized recommendations, making information retrieval more seamless. AI-driven search can predict user intent, assist with research tasks, and streamline knowledge discovery. I recently upgraded my iPhone, and Apple's AI-powered features are already integrated, summarizing my emails and more. At the time of writing, I'm still unsure whether I like this upgrade—it will probably just take some getting used to. If you're like me, your phone feels like an extension of yourself, making any change feel more disruptive than in other areas of life. Adjusting to a new interface or functionality can initially be jarring, but these AI enhancements may prove invaluable.

Despite its potential, AI search faces challenges such as bias, accuracy concerns, and transparency in AI-generated responses. Maintaining reliability and fairness in information presentation will be paramount as AI search evolves.

## FAST-LEARNING ROBOTS: THE NEXT LEAP IN AI-POWERED AUTOMATION

Recent advancements in generative AI and reinforcement learning (RL) enable robots to learn new tasks autonomously and adapt to dynamic environments. Warehouse robots now utilize RL algorithms to recognize objects, optimize packing strategies, and adjust to inventory changes in real time. Similarly, surgical robots continuously refine their precision by learning from past procedures, improving their movements, and enhancing patient outcomes.

At the same time, embodied AI integrates language processing, sensory input, and decision-making, allowing robots to interact with their surroundings in a more human-like and adaptable manner. By processing diverse sensory data—such as visual, auditory, and tactile inputs—these AI-driven systems make context-aware decisions, improving their functionality in complex, real-world scenarios.

While these technologies boost productivity and safety, they raise concerns about job displacement and ethical deployment. The key challenge will be balancing automation with workforce evolution so that human workers are reskilled and integrated into roles that complement AI capabilities. By encouraging a collaborative relationship between humans and machines, businesses and policymakers can simultaneously drive innovation and address the ethical implications of AI deployment.

## SMALL LANGUAGE MODELS: FASTER, CHEAPER, AND MORE ACCESSIBLE

Unlike their LLM counterparts, small language models (SLMs) require less computing power, making AI more accessible for businesses and personal use. SLMs are being developed for:

- *on-device AI assistants* that function without an internet connection,
- *privacy-focused applications* that process data locally, and
- *business tools* that integrate AI without expensive cloud infrastructure

Trade-offs include reduced knowledge depth and reasoning capabilities, but ongoing research aims to optimize performance while maintaining efficiency.

## LARGE LANGUAGE MODELS THAT REASON

As we explored in Chapter 6, "The evolution of prompt engineering," companies like OpenAI have released new models, including o1 and o3, with enhanced reasoning capabilities. These models are designed to handle complex reasoning tasks, generating structured thought processes before responding. xAI's Grok-3 has also been released, adding competition to this space with advanced problem-solving modes such as "Think" for step-by-step reasoning and "Big Brain" for more demanding cognitive tasks.

These reasoning-capable models can break down complex problems into logical steps, analyze arguments, and explain their reasoning for more nuanced and insightful responses. This shift is transforming fields such as:

- *Scientific discovery*—Assisting in hypothesis generation and literature analysis to accelerate research.
- *Legal analysis*—Enhancing regulatory interpretation and case prediction to support legal professionals.
- *Autonomous decision-making*—Improving business strategy formulation and risk assessment for enterprises.

The emergence of AI systems with robust reasoning abilities represents a shift toward AI collaborating on intellectually demanding tasks rather than merely automating basic functions. As these models evolve, their role in high-level decision-making and problem-solving will undoubtedly expand.

## THE MARCH TOWARD ARTIFICIAL GENERAL INTELLIGENCE

Artificial general intelligence (AGI)—the hypothetical point at which machines possess human-level cognitive abilities—has long been a pursuit of scientists, engineers, and philosophers. Unlike today's AI, which excels in narrow domains, AGI would demonstrate reasoning, learning, and adaptability across a wide range of intellectual tasks, like humans. AGI is not merely an advancement in machine learning but a fundamental shift that could redefine human civilization.

Recent progress in generative AI suggests that the foundational pieces of AGI are taking shape, and this technology could arrive faster than initially thought. OpenAI's latest models, DeepMind's AlphaFold, Google's Gemini, and xAI's latest model Grok-3 exhibit remarkable reasoning, pattern recognition, and multimodal understanding capabilities. These developments raise a profound question: Are we on the brink of an intelligence explosion, or is AGI still an elusive concept beyond our current grasp? Given the significance of AGI to humans, we will spend more time on this topic in the coming sections.

## The Path to AGI: Foundations and Breakthroughs

Advances in key areas of AI research, each addressing critical components necessary for general intelligence, are paving the road to AGI. Generative AI models have demonstrated increasing levels of contextual understanding, memory retention, and decision-making, all of which push the boundaries of machine cognition. Techniques like reinforcement learning, transfer learning, and self-supervised training enable AI to apply knowledge flexibly across domains like humans.

Multimodal AI represents another essential step toward AGI. The ability to synthesize information across different sensory inputs mirrors human perception, bringing AI closer to true generalization. Meta's LLaMA and Google's Gemini exemplify this transition, suggesting that AGI may emerge not from a single breakthrough but through the convergence of multiple AI disciplines.

## The Unresolved Challenges of AGI

Despite these advances, fundamental issues remain. The alignment problem—the difficulty of ensuring that AI systems remain aligned with human values—grows increasingly urgent as AI becomes more autonomous. A misaligned AGI could produce unintended consequences, potentially challenging societal stability, governance, or ethical norms. Many researchers see the "alignment problem" as the most pressing issue in AI development, and institutions like Anthropic and DeepMind have dedicated teams exploring new approaches to reinforce safe behaviors and ethical decision-making in AI systems.

Another obstacle is the interpretability problem. Today's AI operates largely as a "black box," producing decisions that are difficult to dissect or explain. For an AGI to be trusted in critical fields such as law, medicine, and finance, it must be transparent, accountable, and capable of reasoning in ways humans can understand. Without breakthroughs in explainable AI, AGI's decision-making may remain opaque, raising significant and valid concerns about control and governance.

### AGI and Global Power Dynamics

The pursuit of AGI is not merely a scientific endeavor but a geopolitical race with significant implications. Leading AI research hubs—including OpenAI, DeepMind, Google, and Microsoft—are at the forefront, but the competition extends beyond corporate labs. Governments worldwide recognize AGI's strategic importance, investing heavily in research to secure technological leadership. The United States and China are locked in an AI arms race, with both nations pouring billions into AI development, often with military and surveillance applications in mind. The lack of global cooperation in AGI governance heightens concerns over its potential misuse. Would AGI be a tool for societal advancement or a mechanism for control and dominance? This question underscores the need for international frameworks that promote transparency, safety, and ethical deployment of AGI. Civil society organizations and global partnerships have also begun advocating for more inclusive, transparent oversight, underscoring that AGI's impact could extend to every sector and social group.

### Preparing for an AGI Future

*If AGI is realized, will humanity be ready?* AGI's implications stretch far beyond technological progress. AGI could transform economies, redefine labor markets, and upend traditional governance structures. Yes, it could accelerate scientific discovery, solving problems once thought intractable, such as disease eradication and resource optimization. Yet, without careful foresight, AGI could also exacerbate economic inequality, disrupt global stability, and introduce ethical dilemmas that society is ill-equipped to navigate.

Experts' views on when AGI might emerge vary widely. Some believe it could happen in a decade or less, while others argue it might take many decades if it happens at all. Regardless of the timeline, policymakers, researchers, and global institutions must anticipate the disruptive potential of AGI and establish guardrails before its arrival. Collaborative efforts such as the Partnership on AI provide a template for responsible AI development; however, a far more comprehensive strategy is needed to make sure AGI serves humanity rather than undermines it.

## FINAL THOUGHTS: GENERATIVE AI'S TRANSFORMATIVE PATH

The challenge ahead is not just technological but also ethical and societal. We must take all necessary steps and precautions to make sure AI enhances human life, including addressing concerns about bias, security, and its societal and economic impacts.

The next era of generative AI will bring more intelligent, autonomous systems that shape industries, scientific breakthroughs, and personal experiences in ways we are only beginning to imagine. As these innovations unfold, the focus must remain on responsible development to maximize benefits while mitigating risks.

* * *

## CHAPTER 13 SELF-ASSESSMENT

Test your knowledge and understanding of this chapter—scan the QR code to the right to access a short quiz. If you prefer entering a link into your browser, here it is: [**https://tinyurl.com/GenAI-Ch13-Quiz**]

QR code to access the Chapter 13 quiz.

# FOURTEEN
# KEEPING UP WITH AI

Keeping up with advancements in AI can feel overwhelming; however, staying informed isn't optional if you want to keep pace with this rapidly evolving, massively impactful technology. This chapter explores practical ways to stay updated, focusing specifically on the tools and resources that can help you navigate the exciting yet complex world of generative AI.

## RELIABLE NEWS SOURCES

In the age of information overload, having trusted news outlets is key to staying informed. Platforms like MIT Technology Review offer robust coverage of advancements in generative AI, such as the implications of tools like ChatGPT or Stable Diffusion across industries like healthcare, marketing, and education. Their reporting often blends technical insights with real-world implications, making it a must-read for professionals and enthusiasts alike. MIT Technology Review frequently highlights breakthroughs while delving into these technologies' societal and ethical implications.

Another excellent resource is The AI Weekly Newsletter, which curates the most significant generative AI news each week and delivers it directly to your inbox. It covers everything from groundbreaking research to practical applications.

"Flying newspapers." AI-generated image using the Open Art platform.

For a broader industry perspective, VentureBeat's AI section is a valuable resource for monitoring how businesses adopt generative AI to streamline operations and enhance productivity. They also provide insight into startup innovations and the competitive landscape.

WIRED is a reputable source for in-depth reporting on AI and its intersection with technology, culture, and society. Their dedicated artificial intelligence section offers many articles covering the latest AI developments, ethical considerations, and industry trends. For a comprehensive understanding of AI, WIRED's Guide to Artificial Intelligence provides an extensive overview of the field, including its history, applications, and prospects. Additionally, WIRED maintains an AI Database that compiles all their AI-related stories so readers can explore content filtered by application, end user, sector, source data, and technology.

Several other reputable platforms provide comprehensive coverage of artificial intelligence developments, including these:

- *IEEE Spectrum* is the flagship magazine of the Institute of Electrical and Electronics Engineers. It offers in-depth articles on various technological topics, including AI. Its coverage includes emerging research, industry trends, and insightful analyses, making it a valuable resource for professionals and enthusiasts alike.
- *AI News* reports on the latest AI news and insights, covering industry trends from the forefront of artificial intelligence. It provides timely updates on technological

advancements, policy changes, and significant events shaping the AI landscape.
- *Rest of World* is a nonprofit journalism organization covering technology's impact, including AI, far beyond the Western bubble. It offers stories and perspectives from regions often underrepresented in mainstream tech media, providing a more global view of AI's influence.

## BLOGS AND THOUGHT LEADERS

Beyond news, insights from thought leaders in the generative AI space are indispensable. OpenAI's Research Blog delves deep into the methodologies behind their models, including their latest GPT and DALL-E releases, providing transparency and technical clarity.

Dr. Andrew Ng, a globally recognized leader in artificial intelligence who was named one of the most influential AI persons in the world in 2023, offers valuable insights in "Andrews Letters," which are personal messages to the AI community, and weekly issues of "The Batch" provide updates on what matters most in AI right now. He frequently discusses how generative AI tools can transform workflows and industries, and his insights into democratizing AI education and applications for non-technical professionals make his posts an excellent starting point for practical guidance.

Another invaluable resource is EleutherAI, a grassroots organization that offers insights into open-source generative AI tools and their development. Their blog updates readers on open-source alternatives competing with commercial giants.

You can also get up-to-date information from researchers and thought leaders in generative AI on social media sites such as LinkedIn and X. Some top AI influencers are listed in Tables 9 and 10 on the following pages.

* * *

**Table 9: Top AI influencers, part 1.**

| Influencer | Role | Foci | Social Media Platforms |
|---|---|---|---|
| **Sam Altman** | CEO of OpenAi | Generative AI advancements, AI safety, AI regulation | @sama on X |
| **Dario Amodei** | CEO and Co-founder of Anthropic | AI safety, generative AI alignment | LinkedIn, @DarioAmodei on X |
| **Yoshua Bengio** | AI Researcher and Professor at the Université de Montréal, multiple honors and awards (e.g., Officer of the Order of Canada (2017), ACM A.M. Turing Award (2018), ACM Fellow (2023)) | Deep learning, AI for societal good, ethics | LinkedIn, @Yoshua_Bengio on X |
| **Heather Dowdy** | VP of Responsible AI at Stability AI | Ethical AI practices, inclusivity in AI development, AI addressing the needs of underrepresented communities, fairness and accountability | LinkedIn, @heatherdowdy on X |
| **Geoffrey Hinton** | AI pioneer (known as the "Godfather of Artificial Intelligence), winner of The Nobel Prize in Physics (2024), neural networks researcher | Deep learning generative models, the future of AI, ethical implications | @geoffreyhinton on X |
| **Fei-Fei Li** | Co-Founder and CEO of World Labs, AI researcher and professor at Stanford University, Co-Director of the Stanford Human-Centered AI Institute (HAI), Co-Founder and Chairperson of the Board at AI4ALL, author of *The Worlds I See* | Human-centered AI, ethical AI, computer vision, robotics, AI in healthcare | LinkedIn, @drfeifei on X |

**Table 10: Top AI influencers, part 2.**

| Influencer | Role | Foci | Social Media Platforms |
|---|---|---|---|
| **Cade Metz** | Technology reporter at The New York Times | Generative AI industry trends, innovations, societal impacts | LinkedIn, @CadeMetz on X |
| **Margaret (Meg) Mitchell** | Researcher and Chief Ethics Scientist at Hugging Face | Machine learning, ethical AI, fairness in generative models | LinkedIn, @mmitchell_ai |
| **Emad Mostaque** | CEO and Founder of Stability AI | Democratizing AI, transparency in AI technologies | LinkedIn, @EMostaque on X |
| **Andrew Ng** | Founder of DeepLearning.AI, Executive Chairman of Landing AI, General Partner at AI Fund, Co-Founder and Chairman of Coursera, Adjunct Professor at Stanford University's Computer Science Department | Deep learning, democratizing AI education, practical applications of AI, generative models | LinkedIn, @AndrewYNg on X |
| **Ilya Sutskever** | Co-founder and Chief Scientist at Safe Superintelligence Inc. | Machine learning, neural networks, safe superintelligence, deep learning | LinkedIn, @ilyasut on X |

## GENERATIVE AI RESEARCH

Staying informed about the latest generative AI research is more manageable with platforms like arXiv, an open-access archive hosting nearly 2.4 million scholarly articles across various fields, including computer science. The platform offers early access to preprints on topics such as prompt engineering, diffusion models, and text-to-image synthesis. For instance, you can find research papers discussing efficiency improvements in models like GPT-4 Turbo, including studies on its effectiveness in generating educational content and enhancing equity in health modeling.

Google Scholar is another valuable tool for tracking academic advancements in generative AI. You can search for studies on LLMs or creative AI applications to uncover cutting-edge findings that inform the broader field.

## CRITICAL THINKING MATTERS

While the resources and tools discussed earlier are invaluable, they are only as good as your ability to critically evaluate the information they provide. Generative AI's complexity often leads to sensationalized or misleading claims, distorting public understanding and influencing decision-making.

"Critical thinker." Generated using DALL-E.

For example, widespread claims have been that AI will "replace entire creative teams overnight," which has not happened, creating unnecessary alarm and hype. These narratives often overlook that generative AI tools like text-to-image or text-to-video systems still rely heavily on human input, oversight, and guidance to produce meaningful results. Such claims also fail to address these tools' limitations and collaborative nature, often requiring refinement to meet the desired outcomes.

When interacting with generative AI content, foundational questions can help guide your evaluation, such as, "Who created this information?" and "What evidence supports it?" Official resources from leading AI developers often clarify the capabilities and constraints of their tools, highlighting how human creativity and technical understanding remain essential components. Understanding biases inherent in training datasets can also explain why generative AI models sometimes produce culturally skewed or exclusionary outputs. Recognizing these nuances empowers you to distinguish between credible claims and overhyped narratives.

Critical thinking is a skill that requires ongoing refinement. Adopting a skeptical but curious mindset allows you to navigate the AI landscape responsibly and avoid falling victim to hype or misinformation.

* * *

## CHAPTER 14 SELF-ASSESSMENT

Keep the momentum going! Go to this link: [**https://tinyurl.com/GenAI-Ch14-Quiz**], or scan the QR code to check your understanding of this chapter.

QR code to access the Chapter 14 quiz.

# BONUS CHAPTERS

As a thank you for purchasing and engaging with this book, I've included three digitally accessible bonus chapters.

## BONUS CHAPTER 1: RESOURCES FOR CONTINUED LEARNING

Explore a curated list of resources for continued learning (including those referenced in Chapter 14), such as news sources, blogs, community engagement platforms, online forums, and more. Scanning the QR code to the right will take you there, or you can enter [**https://tinyurl.com/GenAIBonusResources**] into your browser.

QR code for Bonus Chapter 1.

"Futuristic Library." AI-generated using Midjourney, edited in Canva.

## BONUS CHAPTER 2: FUTURE-READY SKILLS FOR AN AI-DRIVEN WORLD

Learn about the essential competencies required for an increasingly AI-driven world, from critical thinking and adaptability to AI literacy and ethical decision-making. You can access this bonus chapter via the QR code to the right or by entering this URL in your browser: [**https://tinyurl.com/GenAIBonusFutureSkills**].

QR code to access Bonus Chapter 2.

## BONUS CHAPTER 3: PLAN FOR AND EXCEL IN A CAREER IN GENERATIVE AI

QR code to access Bonus Chapter 3.

The rise of AI is changing the labor market and creating career opportunities in AI across industries, but navigating this evolving field requires strategy, adaptability, and the right skill set. This chapter provides a roadmap for building a successful career in AI, from understanding key roles—from AI Research Scientist to Machine Learning Engineer, Natural Language Processing Engineer, AI Ethicist, and more. Whether you're looking to enter the AI field, transition into a new role, or future-proof your career, this chapter will help you identify the best path forward and position yourself for success. To access this content, scan the QR code to the left or enter the URL into your browser: [**https://tinyurl.com/GenAIBonusAICareers**].

# CONCLUSION

Generative AI represents a new frontier in technology, creativity, and problem-solving, and I hope this book has helped you see its potential in your personal and professional life. Whether you came to this book as a curious beginner or someone looking to deepen your understanding, you've taken an important step toward proficiency in one of the most transformative technologies of our time.

Together, we've explored the foundational concepts of generative AI, its real-world applications, and its ability to redefine industries and empower individuals. From generating lifelike images and crafting innovative text to building interactive tools and imagining entirely new possibilities, this journey has explored the power of creation itself.

But this journey is not just about building—it is also about understanding. Throughout this book, we've tackled complex ethical considerations, from ensuring fairness and mitigating bias to protecting privacy and promoting accountability. These discussions underscore a critical truth: *the future of generative AI lies in how congruously we use it.* As creators, innovators, and users of this technology, the responsibility for shaping its impact is ours.

Generative AI offers nearly infinite possibilities. Whether you see yourself improving your productivity at work, changing careers, pursuing creative endeavors, designing ethical AI policies, or launching your own AI-supported business, the opportunities are vast and exciting. What matters most is staying curious and embracing learning as a lifelong process. This book has been a beginning, but your journey continues. With the tools, strategies, and insights you've gained, you're well-equipped to explore the horizons of generative AI and keep up with the latest technological advancements.

As we conclude, I want to leave you with some final thoughts. First, generative AI is not just a tool for efficiency—it's a springboard for innovation, creativity, and addressing local and global challenges. Use it to amplify your ideas, tackle tough problems, and make a meaningful impact. Second, while AI's capabilities are extraordinary, human creativity, empathy, and vision give it purpose. Third, have fun exploring and using this technology; enjoy using it for serious and unserious matters. Finally, remember that this moment is just the beginning of your journey with generative AI. Keep asking questions, experimenting, and challenging yourself.

Maya Angelou (1928–2014) was an acclaimed American poet, memoirist, singer, dancer, actress, and civil rights activist best known for her autobiographical series, beginning with *I Know Why the Caged Bird Sings* (1969). She believed creativity thrives when nurtured with focus and purpose and grows stronger through consistent use. She famously said,

> *"You can't use up creativity. The more you use, the more you have."*

Let Angelou's words inspire you as you continue exploring, learning, and building with generative AI.

Thank you for choosing me to guide you through this exciting and timely topic. I hope it has ignited your curiosity and confidence to shape the future with generative AI.

# THANK YOU!

Thank you for reading *Generative AI Basics & Beyond*! I hope you found it valuable and enjoyed it as much as I enjoyed writing it.

If you haven't already, I'd truly appreciate it if you left a review. Your feedback helps others discover the book—and it might just make a meaningful difference in their personal and professional lives.

***Your review takes seconds but can guide someone toward a game-changing discovery!***

Please scan the QR code below to leave your review, or enter this link into your browser: [**https://geni.us/GenAIReviewPB**]

*With gratitude,*
*Melissa*

QR code to leave a review.

# REFERENCES


Abakcus. (2023, October 20). *18 Remarkable women in STEM who changed the world.* https://abakcus.com/18-remarkable-women-in-stem/

AI Filmmaking [ai filmmaking]. (n.d.). Runway Gen 3: The Future of AI Filmmaking. *Filmart ai.* https://filmart.ai/runway-gen-3/

*AI, tech and the intelligent age at Davos 2025: What to know.* (2025, January 30). World Economic Forum. https://www.weforum.org/stories/2025/01/industries-in-the-intelligent-age-ai-tech-theme-davos-2025/

Akerman, I. (2023, December 27). *Voice cloning is infiltrating our digital life. WIRED Middle East.* https://wired.me/technology/voice-cloning-ai/

Alex. (2024, November 10). *8 Best Tools to Detect AI-Generated Videos & Deepfakes in 2025.* https://usefulai.com/tools/ai-video-detectors

*Algorithmic Justice League - Unmasking AI harms and biases.* (n.d.). https://www.ajl.org/

*Aman's AI Journal • Primers • Evaluation Metrics.* (n.d.). https://aman.ai/primers/ai/evaluation-metrics/

Amazon. (2018, May 30). *Expanding the Natural-Language Processing community.* https://www.aboutamazon.com/news/innovation-at-amazon/expanding-the-natural-language-processing-community

Aoi + Esteban. (2024). *LILITH.AEON - Aoi + Esteban.* https://aoiesteban.com/project/lilithaeon/

Aqua. (2023, December 3). Chat GPT revolutionizes the landscape of higher education by enhancing student engagement and learning experience. *Aquarius.* https://aquariusai.ca/blog/chat-gpt-revolutionizes-the-landscape-of-higher-education-by enhancing-student-engagement-and-learning-experience

Arzomand, K., Rutsell, M., & Kalganova, T. (2024). From ruins to reconstruction: Harnessing text-to-image AI for restoring historical architectures. *Challenge Journal of Structural Mechanics, 10*(2). https://www.challengejournal.com/index.php/cjsmec/article/view/797

Ashraf, M., & Bocca, R. (2024). Fostering Effective Energy Transition Insight Report. In *World Economic Forum.* https://www3.weforum.org/docs/WEF_Fostering_Effective_Energy_Transition_2024.pdf

Ashworth, B. (2024a, July 30). Wear this AI friend around your neck. *WIRED.* https://www.wired.com/story/friend-ai-pendant/

Ashworth, B. (2024b, August 28). The Plaud NotePin is an AI notetaker that will transcribe your meetings—and your entire life. *WIRED.* https://www.wired.com/story/plaud-note-pin-ai-wearable/

Authors A.I. (n.d.). *Meet Marlowe: The self-editing tool.* https://authors.ai/marlowe/

Azagury, J., Grant, K. F., Moore, M., Ashraf, M., Accenture, & Moore, M. (n.d.). Reinvention in the age of generative AI. In *Accenture.* https://www.accenture.com/content/dam/accenture/final/accenture-com/document-2/Accenture-Reinvention-in-the-age-of-generative-AI-Report.pdf#zoom=40

Banias, M. (2024, February 1). *AI image generator Midjourney is accidentally creating NSFW content, violating its own guidelines. The Debrief.* https://thedebrief.org/ai-image-generator-midjourney-is-accidentally-creating-nsfw-content-violating-its-own-guidelines/

*Barbara J. Grosz.* (n.d.). Harvard University. https://grosz.seas.harvard.edu/

Barrabi, T. (2025, February 18). Elon Musk's xAI claims newest Grok 3 model outperforms OpenAI, DeepSeek. *New York Post.* https://nypost.com/2025/02/18/business/elon-musks-xai-claims-grok-3-outperforms-openai-deepseek/

Basti W. (2024, February). *AI Video - 10 month difference. And now OpenAI and Sora!* [Video]. YouTube. https://www.youtube.com/watch?v=3P1fDaDQ7Io

Bates, C. (2024, March 23). *10 Generative AI skills You need to succeed in 2024.* Dataquest. https://www.dataquest.io/blog/10-generative-ai-skills-you-need-to-succeed/

BBC News. (2024, March). *How AI and deepfakes are changing politics* [Video]. YouTube. https://www.youtube.com/watch?v=wxEpPin8MWw

Beaty, T. (2024, November 22). *AI could help scale humanitarian responses. But it could also have big downsides.* AP News. https://apnews.com/article/international-rescue-committee-ai-refugees-chatbots-9c5fae949c429c38019feabaeec5fafa

Belanger, A. (2024, September 25). DoNotPay has to pay $193K for falsely touting untested AI lawyer, FTC says. *Ars Technica.* https://arstechnica.com/tech-policy/2024/09/startup-behind-worlds-first-robot-lawyer-to-pay-193k-for-false-ads-ftc-says/

Beres, D. (2024, October 4). What If your ChatGPT transcripts leaked? *The Atlantic.* https://www.theatlantic.com/newsletters/archive/2024/10/what-if-your-chatgpt-transcripts-leaked/680165/

Bhupatiraju, S. (2024, September 2). Evaluating Generative AI models: metrics, methods, and best practices. *Ecorfy.* https://ecorfy.com/2024/09/02/evaluating-generative-ai-models-metrics-methods-and-best-practices/

Bindman, D. (2023, February 16). Ask me anything – Allen & Overy adopts ChatGPT-style legal AI tool. *Legal Futures.* https://www.legalfutures.co.uk/latest-news/ask-me-anything-allen-overy-adopts-chatgpt-style-legal-ai-tool

*BMW Group, Airbus and Quantinuum joined forces and achieved breakthrough in quantum science - utilization of quantum computers to contribute to future sustainable mobility.* (2023, February 8). [Press release]. BMW Group PressClub. https://www.press.bmwgroup.com/global/article/detail/T0426579EN/bmw-group-airbus-and-quantinuum-collaborate-to-fast-track-sustainable-mobility-research-using-cutting-edge-quantum-computers?language=en

*BMW Group and Pasqal expand Collaboration to apply Quantum Computing to improve Car Design and Manufacturing - Pasqal.* (2022, May 11). [Press release]. Pasqal. https://www.pasqal.com/news/bmw-group-and-pasqal-expand-collaboration-to-apply-quantum-computing-to-improve-car-design-and-manufacturing/

Borak, M. (2024, December 6). DoD awards contract for deepfake detection to Hive. *Biometric Update | Biometrics News, Companies and Explainers.* https://www.biometricupdate.com/202412/dod-awards-contract-for-deepfake-detection-to-hive

Born to Engineer. (2023, March). *20 Historic Female Engineers Who Shaped Our World: Honoring Their Achievements On International Women's.* https://www.borntoengineer.com/historic-female-engineers-shaping-our-world-international-womens-day

Bretous, M. (2024, December 17). Real or AI-Generated? You Guess [Quiz]. *HubSpot.* https://blog.hubspot.com/marketing/real-or-ai

Bulakh, A. (2024, April 9). Ethics in AI: Making voice cloning safe. *Respeecher.* https://www.respeecher.com/news/ethics-in-ai-making-voice-cloning-safe

Cagle, P. (2024, March 14). *5 AI Case Studies in Education.* VKTR. https://www.vktr.com/ai-disruption/5-ai-case-studies-in-education/

Carr, A., Day, M., Frier, S., & Gurman, M. (2019, December 11). Silicon Valley Is Listening to Your Most Intimate Moments. *Bloomberg.* https://www.bloomberg.com/news/features/2019-12-11/silicon-valley-got-millions-to-let-siri-and-alexa-listen-in?embedded-checkout=true

CBC News: The National. (2024, January 17). *Can you spot the deepfake? How AI is threatening elections* [Video]. YouTube. https://www.youtube.com/watch?v=B4jNttRvbpU

Chan, B., et al. (2024, December 28). *Here's everything we know about how Wall Street banks are embracing AI.* Business Insider. https://www.businessinsider.com/everything-we-know-about-how-banks-using-ai-2024-8

Chang, J. (2023). *The application of generative adversarial networks in cultural heritage preservation.* IEEE Conference Publication | IEEE Xplore. https://ieeexplore.ieee.org/document/10336478

Chatterjee, S., Desarkar, A., Raman, V., & LTIMindtree. (n.d.). *The power of Generative AI in Predictive Maintenance: Exploring equipment failure cases* [Online]. LTIMindtree. https://www.ltimindtree.com/wp-content/uploads/2024/04/The-Power-of-Generative-AI-in-Predictive-Maintenance.pdf

Chen, R., et al. (2023). Generative design of outdoor green spaces based on generative adversarial networks. *Buildings, 13*(4), 1083. https://doi.org/10.3390/buildings13041083

Chesnokova, S. (2025, February 13). *$50M for AI-programmable biology: Latent Labs, led by DeepMind's AlphaFold alumnus, to design novel proteins.* Tech Funding News. https://techfundingnews.com/50m-for-ai-programmable-biology-latent-labs-led-by-deepminds-alphafold-alumnus-to-design-novel-proteins/

Chobey, R. D. (2024, October 3). Google for India 2024: Making the promise of AI real for individuals, society and the economy. *Google.* https://blog.google/intl/en-in/company-news/outreach-initiatives/google-for-india-2024-making-the-promise-of-ai-real-for-individuals-society-and-the-economy/

Choi, S. L., et al. (2024). Generative AI for power grid operations. In *National Renewable Energy Laboratory (NREL)* (Technical Report NREL/TP-5D09-91176). National Renewable Energy Laboratory. https://www.nrel.gov/docs/fy25osti/91176.pdf

Chow, A. R. (2024, October 31). Inside the new nonprofit AI initiatives seeking to aid teachers and farmers in rural Africa. *TIME.* https://time.com/7160849/opportunity-international-ai-farmers-teachers/

CNN. (2024). *We showed people an AI political ad. Can they tell it's fake?* [Video]. YouTube. https://www.youtube.com/watch?v=-0ZFgjELb8w

Colverd, G., Darm, P., Silverberg, L., & Kasmanoff, N. (2023). FloodBrain: Flood Disaster Reporting by Web-based Retrieval Augmented Generation with an LLM. *arXiv.org.* https://doi.org/10.48550/arXiv.2311.02597

*Content Authenticity Initiative*. (n.d.). https://contentauthenticity.org/

Cornell University. (n.d.). *arXiv.org e-Print archive*. arXiv. https://arxiv.org/

Cost, B. (2024, May 7). AI voice scammers are posing as loved ones to steal your money — here's a foolproof trick to stop attacks. *New York Post*. https://nypost.com/2024/05/07/tech/ai-voice-scammers-are-posing-as-loved-ones-to-steal-your-money-heres-a-foolproof-trick-to-stop-attacks/

Cotruta, C. (2024, September 30). *The role of AI in Residential Housing Projects: A path to Sustainable solutions*. Archinect. https://archinect.com/cotrutacristina/the-role-of-ai-in-residential-housing-projects-a-path-to-sustainable-solutions

Data4Energy. (2024, October 14). *AI-Powered Predictive Maintenance: Transforming turbine management in 2024*. Data for Energy. https://data4energy.com/ai-powered-predictive-maintenance-transforming-turbine-management-in-2024

David, E. (2024, December 30). Why 2025 will be the year of AI orchestration. *VentureBeat*. https://venturebeat.com/ai/three-ways-2025-will-be-the-year-of-agentic-productivity/

Day, M. (2023, June 1). Thirty Thousand Amazon Workers Could Access Alexa Data, FTC Says. *Bloomberg*. https://www.bloomberg.com/news/articles/2023-06-01/thirty-thousand-amazon-workers-could-access-alexa-data-ftc-says

Deepgram. (n.d.-a). *AI Voice Detector*. https://deepgram.com/ai-apps/ai-voice-detector

Deepgram. (n.d.-b). *Reprompt: Collaborative AI Prompt Testing Platform*. https://deepgram.com/ai-apps/reprompt

Diep Nep. (2021, July 7). *This is not Morgan Freeman - A Deepfake Singularity* [Video]. YouTube. https://www.youtube.com/watch?v=oxXpB9pSETo

DigitalDefynd. (2024). *20 Generative AI Case Studies [2024]*. https://digitaldefynd.com/IQ/generative-ai-case-studies/

Digital Ocean (n.d.) *10 AI music Generators for Creators in 2024*. https://www.digitalocean.com/resources/articles/ai-music-generators

Dilmegani, C. D. (2024, December 10). *Top 100+ Generative AI Applications with Real-Life Examples*. AIMultiple Research. https://research.aimultiple.com/generative-ai-applications/

Doukas, A. (2023, January 27). *Introducing Copilot and AlphaCode: Understanding the differences and similarities*. Solwey Consulting. https://www.solwey.com/posts/introducing-copilot-and-alphacode-understanding-the-differences-and-similarities#:~:text=Both%20Copilot%20and%20AlphaCode%20are,speed%20up%20the%20development%20process.

Duolingo. (2023, March 14). Duolingo Max uses OpenAI's GPT-4 for new learning features. *Duolingo Blog*. https://blog.duolingo.com/duolingo-max/

Eaton Corporation plc & aPriori. (2024). *Eaton's generative AI cuts product design time by 87 percent*. aPriori. https://www.apriori.com/wp-content/uploads/2024/08/Eaton_and_aPriori-Case-Study-V3.pdf

Edwards, B. (2022, December 15). Stability AI plans to let artists opt out of Stable Diffusion 3 image training. *Ars Technica*. https://arstechnica.com/information-technology/2022/12/stability-ai-plans-to-let-artists-opt-out-of-stable-diffusion-3-image-training/

Edwards, P. H. &. C. (2025, January 28). *Nvidia and Microsoft shares steady after DeepSeek AI app shock.* https://www.bbc.com/news/articles/c4gpq01rvd4o

Ekeopara, P., & Nekekpemi, P. (2024). Generative AI: Prospects and applications in geothermal energy. In *PROCEEDINGS, 49th Workshop on Geothermal Reservoir Engineering: Vol. SGP-TR-227.* https://pangea.stanford.edu/ERE/db/GeoConf/papers/SGW/2024/Ekeopara.pdf

EleutherAI. (n.d.). *EleutherAI.* https://www.eleuther.ai/

ElevenLabs. (n.d.). *Detect whether an audio clip was created using ElevenLabs | ElevenLabs.* https://elevenlabs.io/ai-speech-classifier

ElevenLabs & Loccus. (2023, October 6). *ElevenLabs and Loccus launch collaboration on Deepfake.* ElevenLabs. https://elevenlabs.io/blog/elevenlabs-and-loccus-launch-collaboration-on-deepfake-detection-systems

Ellencweig, B., Mysore, M., & Spaner, J. (2023, October 17). *Generative AI is set to transform crisis management.* Nextgov.com. https://www.nextgov.com/ideas/2023/10/generative-ai-set-transform-crisis-management/391264/

Esser, J. (2025, January 15). Embodied AI explained: principles, applications, and future perspectives. *Lamarr Institute for Machine Learning and Artificial Intelligence.* https://lamarr-institute.org/blog/embodied-ai-explained/

Fan, Q., & Qiang, C. Z. (2024, June 3). Tipping the scales: AI's dual impact on developing nations. *World Bank Blogs.* https://blogs.worldbank.org/en/digital-development/tipping-the-scales--ai-s-dual-impact-on-developing-nations

Farid, H. (n.d.). *Quiz: AI or not.* Berkeley. https://farid.berkeley.edu/misc/AIorNotQuiz/

FBI. (2024, December 3). *Criminals use generative artificial intelligence to facilitate financial fraud.* Federal Bureau of Investigation (FBI) Internet Crime Complaint Center. https://www.ic3.gov/PSA/2024/PSA241203

Federation of State Medical Boards [FSMB]. (2024a). Navigating the Responsible and Ethical Incorporation of Artificial Intelligence into Clinical Practice. In *Federation of State Medical Boards (FSMB).* https://www.fsmb.org/siteassets/advocacy/policies/incorporation-of-ai-into-practice.pdf

Federation of State Medical Boards [FSMB]. (2024b, May 2). *FSMB Releases Recommendations on the Responsible and Ethical Incorporation of AI into Clinical Practice* [Press release]. https://www.fsmb.org/advocacy/news-releases/fsmb-releases-recommendations-on-the-responsible-and-ethical-incorporation-of-ai-into-clinical-practice/

Firstpost. (2022, September 5). Explained: The controversy surrounding the AI-generated artwork that won US competition. *Firstpost.* https://www.firstpost.com/explainers/explained-the-controversy-surrounding-the-ai-generated-artwork-that-won-us-competition-11188431.html

Frazier, K., Rozenshtein, A., & Salib, P. (2024, December 23). *OpenAI's latest model shows AGI is inevitable. Now what?* Default. https://www.lawfaremedia.org/article/openai%27s-latest-model-shows-agi-is-inevitable.-now-what

From Narrow To General AI. (2024, May 8). Why AI-generated videos feel hypnotic, fluid, and uncanny. *Medium.* https://ykulbashian.medium.com/why-ai-generated-videos-feel-hypnotic-fluid-and-uncanny-71c822ad3da5

Gartner. (2024, September 9). *Gartner Predicts 40% of Generative AI Solutions Will Be*

*Multimodal By 2027* [Press release]. https://www.gartner.com/en/newsroom/press-releases/2024-09-09-gartner-predicts-40-percent-of-generative-ai-solutions-will-be-multimodal-by-2027

Ge, X., Goodwin, R. T., Yu, H., Romero, P., Abdelrahman, O., Sudhalkar, A., Kusuma, J., Cialdella, R., Garg, N., & Varshney, L. R. (2022, April 11). *Accelerated design and deployment of Low-Carbon concrete for data centers*. arXiv.org. https://arxiv.org/abs/2204.05397

Get to the Point. (2023, February 1). *AI vs Human Songs Quiz, Can you guess all 10? Google's MusicLM AI makes music from text prompts.* [Video]. YouTube. https://www.youtube.com/watch?v=RDOJJrOJ0Zs

Golemanova, R. (2017, June 1). 11 female researchers who made a big impact on artificial intelligence. *Imagga Blog.* https://imagga.com/blog/11-female-researchers-made-big-impact-artifical-intelligence/

Gonzalez-Delgado, D., Jaen-Sola, P., & Oterkus, E. (2024). Generative Design and Additive Manufacturing Techniques on the Optimization of Multi-MW Offshore Direct-Drive Wind Turbine Electrical Generators. In *The 4th Annual Conference Solar and Wind Power* (1st ed., Vol. 71, p. 4). https://doi.org/10.3390/engproc2024071004

Gordon, R. (2023, July 12). *Generative AI imagines new protein structures.* MIT News | Massachusetts Institute of Technology. https://news.mit.edu/2023/generative-ai-imagines-new-protein-structures-0712

Governor Gavin Newsom. (2024, September 5). *Governor Newsom seeks to harness the power of GenAI to address homelessness, other challenges* [Press release]. Governor of California. https://www.gov.ca.gov/2024/09/05/governor-newsom-seeks-to-harness-the-power-of-genai-to-address-homelessness-other-challenges/

Grantham-Philips, W. (2024, December 30). *AI is becoming ingrained in businesses across industries. Where is it going in 2025?* AP News. https://apnews.com/article/artificial-intelligence-interview-pwc-dan-priest-a04580614697 35aed7af5fa49682e076

Grunert, J. (n.d.). *GenAI Use Cases and Best Practices: A CIO's Perspective.* rSTAR Technologies Blog. https://rstartec.com/insights/genai-use-cases-and-best-practices-a-cio-perspective/

Guinness, H. (2024, September 18). *The 7 best AI image generators in 2024.* Zapier. https://zapier.com/blog/best-ai-image-generator/

Hawke, S. (2025, January). *Generative AI in Healthcare: Transforming the future of patient care.* 01. https://vocal.media/01/generative-ai-in-healthcare-transforming-the-future-of-patient-care

Heikkilä, M. (2022, December 19). How to spot AI-generated text. *MIT Technology Review.* https://www.technologyreview.com/2022/12/19/1065596/how-to-spot-ai-generated-text/

Hiya. (n.d.). *Deepfake voice detector.* https://www.hiya.com/products/deepfake-voice-detector

Holmes, T. (2024, February 20). *How to prepare for generative AI and the future of work.* PluralSight. https://www.pluralsight.com/resources/blog/ai-and-data/generative-ai-future-of-work

Horsey, J. (2024a, March 18). *A closer look at Rabbit R1 and Humane Ai Pin wearables.* Geeky Gadgets. https://www.geeky-gadgets.com/ai-wearables/

*How is natural language processing empowering women in tech?* (n.d.). Women in Tech Network. https://www.womentech.net/en-us/how-to/how-natural-language-processing-empowering-women-in-tech

HPCwire. (2023, February 9). *SEEQC Partners with BASF to Explore Applications of Quantum Computing in Chemical Reactions for Industrial Use.* https://www.hpcwire.com/off-the-wire/seeqc-partners-with-basf-to-explore-applications-of-quantum-computing-in-chemical-reactions-for-industrial-use/

Hugging Face. (n.d.). *The AI community building the future.* https://huggingface.co/

IBM. (n.d.). *IBM Watson Studio.* https://www.ibm.com/products/watson-studio

Ikezuruora, C. (2024, February 5). *Wearable tech and personal privacy: Unveiling the hidden risks.* PrivacyEnd. https://www.privacyend.com/wearable-tech-impacts-personal-privacy/

Illuminarty. (n.d.). *AI generated Content Detection - Illuminarty - Home.* https://illuminarty.ai/en/

illustrarch Editorial Team. (2024, December 5). *The Role of AI in Modern Architectural Design.* Illustrarch. https://illustrarch.com/artificial-intelligence/36283-the-role-of-ai-in-modern-architectural-design.html?srsltid=AfmBOoqlNAbTg_CUjiWfevT2TsrFZ_2altF6W4iksW-5a6BzR3b9Aytq

*Images: Evaluating images.* (n.d.). Library Guides. https://guides.lib.uw.edu/c.php?g=344258&p=2318783

Immigration, Refugees and Citizenship Canada. (2024, June 20). *Canada honours and shows solidarity with refugees worldwide.* Government of Canada. https://www.canada.ca/en/immigration-refugees-citizenship/news/2024/06/canada-honours-and-shows-solidarity-with-refugees-worldwide.html

Jin, B. (2025, January 27). Reid Hoffman Raises $24.6 Million for AI Cancer-Research Startup. *Wall Street Journal.* https://www.wsj.com/tech/ai/manas-ai-drug-discovery-reid-hoffman-93a6c023

Johnson, E. (2024, October 9). *Harnessing Generative AI for predictive maintenance | Siemens Blog | Siemens.* Siemens. https://blog.siemens.com/2024/10/harnessing-generative-ai-for-predictive-maintenance/

Joshi, N. (2022, April 14). 7 types of artificial intelligence. *Forbes.* https://www.forbes.com/sites/cognitiveworld/2019/06/19/7-types-of-artificial-intelligence/

Kamble, S., & Mehrotra, S. (2023, November 20). *Accelerating Operational Excellence with Generative AI for Manufacturing, amidst dynamic processes and market conditions.* Birlasoft | CK Birla Group. https://www.birlasoft.com/articles/generativeai-operational-excellence-manufacturing

Kannan, P. (2023, May 9). *Diyi Yang: Human-Centered natural language processing will produce more inclusive technologies.* Stanford University Human-Centered Artificial Intelligence. https://hai.stanford.edu/news/diyi-yang-human-centered-natural-language-processing-will-produce-more-inclusive-technologies

Kannan, P. (2024, October 3). *How harmful are AI's biases on diverse student populations?* Stanford HAI. https://hai.stanford.edu/news/how-harmful-are-ais-biases-diverse-student-populations

Kansal, A., Chawla, S., & Shankar, S. (2023). A multi-tiered approach to debiasing language models. In Stanford CS224N Custom Project, Department of Computer Science, Stanford University, & Department of Electrical Engineering,

Stanford University, *Stanford CS224N Natural Language Processing With Deep Learning* [Thesis]. https://web.stanford.edu/class/archive/cs/cs224n/cs224n.1244/final-projects/AmanKansalSaanviChawlashreyashankar.pdf

Kato, B. (2024, October 4). AI is spying on your workplace gossip and secrets — and sharing them afterward. *New York Post*. https://nypost.com/2024/10/04/tech/ai-is-spying-on-your-workplace-gossip-and-secrets-and-sharing-them-afterward/

Kearney, H. (2024, April 8). Generative AI for better humanitarian programming: A test case. *Medium*. https://medium.com/@h.f.kearney/generative-ai-for-better-humanitarian-programming-a-test-case-eb9ed767bd34

Keller, E. (2023, February 14). David Guetta deepfakes Eminem's voice in new song: 'Future of music is in AI.' *New York Post*. https://nypost.com/2023/02/14/david-guetta-deepfakes-eminems-voice-in-new-song-future-of-music-is-in-ai/

Khanmingo. (n.d.). *Meet Khanmigo: Khan Academy's AI-powered teaching assistant & tutor*. https://www.khanmigo.ai/

Kinde, A. (2024, December 3). *AI's Linguistic Bias: A Silent Architect of Cultural Marginalization?* Mindplex. https://magazine.mindplex.ai/ais-linguistic-bias-a-silent-architect-of-cultural-marginalization/

Kinder, M., Muro, M., & De Souza Briggs, X. (2024, October 10). The AI revolution is coming for your Non-Union job. *TIME*. https://time.com/7081228/ai-non-union-job-essay/

Kirimi, W. (2024, October 21). *How to check for AI-Generated Images: 6 key detection Methods*. ImageSuggest. https://imagesuggest.com/blog/how-to-check-ai-generated-images/

Knight, W. (2025, January 28). DeepSeek's new AI model sparks shock, awe, and questions from US competitors. *WIRED*. https://www.wired.com/story/deepseek-executives-reaction-silicon-valley/

Knight, W. (2024, December 20). OpenAI upgrades its smartest AI model with improved reasoning skills. *WIRED*. https://www.wired.com/story/openai-o3-reasoning-model-google-gemini/

Kuchler, H., & Heikkilä, M. (2025, February 13). Ex-DeepMind scientist launches AI drug discovery venture. *Financial Times*. https://www.ft.com/content/92143d49-c777-4bba-8857-b4ef7e82ebd4?

Krieger, M. M., & Cohen, D. R. (2024, December 20). *Navigating the seven C's of ethical use of AI by lawyers*. Reuters. https://www.reuters.com/legal/legalindustry/navigating-seven-cs-ethical-use-ai-by-lawyers-2024-12-20/

Lamensch, M. (2021, August 11). *Putting our bodies online: The privacy risks of tech wearables*. Centre for International Governance Innovation. https://www.cigionline.org/articles/putting-our-bodies-online-the-privacy-risks-of-tech-wearables/

Lanz, J. A. (2024, December 5). *Tencent's new AI video generator takes on OpenAI's Sora for free*. Decrypt. https://decrypt.co/295199/tencents-new-ai-video-generator-takes-on-openais-sora-for-free

Li, R., Zhang, Y., & Xie, Z. (2024). Evaluating the culture-awareness in pre-trained language model. In Stanford CS224N & Stanford University, *Stanford CS224N Custom Project* [Report]. https://web.stanford.edu/class/archive/cs/cs224n/cs224n.1244/final-projects/RyanLiYutongZhangZhiyuXie.pdf

Lin, C. (2020, November 27). A Timeline of Firsts: Recognizing brave female pioneers in STEM – Yale Scientific Magazine. *Yale Scientific*. https://www.yalescientific.org/2020/11/a-timeline-of-firsts-recognizing-brave-female-pioneers-in-stem/

Lin, Z., et al. (2023). Leveraging Generative AI for Renewable Energy: Photovoltaic Panel Semantic Segmentation Case Study. *Energy Proceedings, 36*. https://doi.org/10.1016/j.adapen.2021.100057

Luminance. (n.d.). *Legal-Grade AI*. https://www.luminance.com/

Luminance. (2024). *Luminance's Legal Pre-Trained Transformer (LPT)*. https://www.luminance.com/technology.html

M, P. [Pavitra M]. (2024, August 22). *10 Mind-Blowing Examples of AI-Generated Art*. ClickUp. https://clickup.com/blog/ai-art-examples/

Mack, D. (2018, April 17). This PSA about fake news from Barack Obama is not what it appears. *BuzzFeed News*. https://www.buzzfeednews.com/article/davidmack/obama-fake-news-jordan-peele-psa-video-buzzfeed

*Magic circle firm rolls out "gamechanger" ChatGPT-type platform*. (2023, February 15). Law Gazette. https://www.lawgazette.co.uk/news/magic-circle-firm-rolls-out-gamechanger-chatgpt-type-platform/5115150.article

Maheshwari, D. (2024, September 2). The Future of Generative AI: A Multi-Year Outlook - Deepak Maheshwari - Medium. *Medium*. https://maheshwari-bittu.medium.com/the-future-of-generative-ai-a-multi-year-outlook-9ecbb7fa1736

*MANAS AI | Disrupting Drug Development*. (n.d.). https://www.manasai.co/

Mark Cuban Companies. (n.d.). *Synthesia - Mark Cuban Companies*. https://markcubancompanies.com/companies/synthesia/

Marr, B. (2023a, July 24). The difference between generative AI and traditional AI: an easy explanation for anyone. *Forbes*. https://www.forbes.com/sites/bernardmarr/2023/07/24/the-difference-between-generative-ai-and-traditional-ai-an-easy-explanation-for-anyone/

Marr, B. (2024, March 5). The future of Generative AI: 6 Predictions Everyone Should Know about. *Forbes*. https://www.forbes.com/sites/bernardmarr/2024/03/05/the-future-of-generative-ai-6-predictions-everyone-should-know-about/

Marshall, M. (2024, December 30). Five breakthroughs that make OpenAI's o3 a turning point for AI — and one big challenge. *VentureBeat*. https://venturebeat.com/ai/five-breakthroughs-that-make-openais-o3-a-turning-point-for-ai-and-one-big-challenge/

Mashette, N. (2025, January 24). Artificial General Intelligence — AGI - Nagesh Mashette - Medium. *Medium*. https://medium.com/%40nageshmashette32/artificial-general-intelligence-agi-2e56242c554d

Martino, M. (2024, September 13). *Artificial intelligence is flooding the internet with fake images, video and audio. Can you tell real from fake?* ABC News. https://www.abc.net.au/news/2024-09-14/artificial-intelligence-real-fake-quiz-abc-news-verify/104148236

Matic. (2024, November 20). *Detecting AI-Generated Text: Things to watch for*. Autogpt. https://autogpt.net/detecting-ai-generated-text-things-to-watch-for/

McFarland, A. (2024a, December 31). *7 Best Deepfake Detector Tools & Techniques (December 2024)*. Unite.AI. https://www.unite.ai/best-deepfake-detector-tools-and-techniques/

McFarland, A. (2024b, December 31). *10 Best AI Video Generators (December 2024)*. Unite.AI. https://www.unite.ai/best-ai-video-generators/

McKay, C. (2025, January 28). *Manas AI launches with $24.6M to tackle cancer through AI-Driven Drug Discovery*. Maginative. https://www.maginative.com/article/manas-ai-launches-with-24-6m-to-tackle-cancer-through-ai-driven-drug-discovery/

McLane, B. (2024, December 17). *How to evaluate Generative AI models: best practices and metrics*. DataStax. https://www.datastax.com/guides/how-to-evaluate-generative-ai-models

*Measuring Development 2024: AI, the next generation*. (2024, May 2). World Bank. https://www.worldbank.org/en/events/2024/05/02/measuring-development-2024

Megorskaya, O. (2024, December 5). AI And Us: The Role Of Human Preference In Model Alignment. *Forbes*. https://www.forbes.com/councils/forbestechcouncil/2024/12/05/ai-and-us-the-role-of-human-preference-in-model-alignment/

Meta. (n.d.). *Meta Movie Gen*. https://ai.meta.com/research/movie-gen/

MG AEC & Autodesk. (n.d.). *Mainstreaming sustainability with generative design capabilities*. Autodesk. https://www.autodesk.com/customer-stories/mg-aec

Mike Haley. (n.d.). The future of making will be powered by generative design and generative AI. *Construction Management Association of America*. https://www.cmaanet.org/sites/default/files/resource/The%20Future%20of%20Making%20UPDATED.pdf

Miliband, D. (2024, December 10). More humanitarian organizations will harness AI's potential. *WIRED*. https://www.wired.com/story/humanitarian-organizations-artificial-intelligence/

Miller, K. (2024, September 3). *Covert racism in AI: How language models are reinforcing outdated stereotypes*. Stanford HAI. https://hai.stanford.edu/news/covert-racism-ai-how-language-models-are-reinforcing-outdated-stereotypes

MIT Media Lab. (n.d.). *Project Overview ‹ Detect DeepFakes: How to counteract misinformation created by AI*. https://www.media.mit.edu/projects/detect-fakes/overview/

Mlot, S. (2023, March 17). Duolingo's Max Subscription Uses GPT-4 for AI-Powered Language Learning. *PC Mag*. https://www.pcmag.com/news/duolingos-max-subscription-uses-gpt-4-for-ai-powered-language-learning

Modi, P. (2024, January 25). *AI won't take your job. somebody who knows how to use AI better than you will take your job*. EducationNext. https://www.educationnext.in/posts/ai-wont-take-your-job-somebody-who-knows-how-to-use-ai-better-than-you-will-take-your-job

Morelo, D. (2024, February 14). *5 ways to Detect AI-Generated Images*. Make Tech Easier. https://www.maketecheasier.com/detect-ai-generated-images/

Morrison Foerster. (2024, October 4). *To scrape or not to scrape? First court decision on the EU copyright exception for text and data mining in Germany*. https://www.mofo.com/resources/insights/241004-to-scrape-or-not-to-scrape-first-court-decision

Mulligan, S. J. (2025, January 3). Generative AI search: 10 Breakthrough Technologies 2025. *MIT Technology Review*. https://www.technologyreview.com/2025/01/03/1108820/generative-ai-search-apple-google-microsoft-breakthrough-technologies-2025/

*Multimedia - the Algorithmic Justice League*. (n.d.). https://www.ajl.org/library/multimedia

Murgia, M., & Gabert-Doyon, J. (2025, February 11). Transcript: Making money from AI — Searching for a 'killer app.' *Financial Times*. https://www.ft.com/content/258bfa07-f43c-459c-82f1-ea61235d73bb

Murgia, M., & Murphy, H. (2024, May 9). TikTok to automatically label AI-generated user content in global first. *Financial Times*. https://www.ft.com/content/658c91f5-9eb2-4863-be0b-ee16ad1bc96c

Murphy, P. (n.d.). *Exploring The Potential of Generative AI to Support The Creation of Homes That are Affordable, Accessible, and Sustainable*. Maket. https://www.maket.ai/post/exploring-the-potential-of-generative-ai-to-support-the-creation-of-homes-that-are-affordable-accessible-and-sustainable

Nelken-Zitser, J. (2024, September 30). *South Korea could give those who watch deepfake porn 3 years in prison or a fine of up to $23K*. Business Insider. https://www.businessinsider.com/south-korea-threatens-deepfake-porn-viewers-three-years-prison-fine-2024-9

Nelson, G. (2024, December 26). ARTnews.com. *ARTnews.com*. https://www.artnews.com/art-news/news/new-magazine-dedicated-to-ai-art-and-what-happens-when-humans-and-machines-get-creative-launches-1234728751/

Nepori, A. (2024, August 2). *The AI-powered Friend is one of the most depressing gadgets we've ever seen*. Domus. https://www.domusweb.it/en/news/gallery/2024/08/01/friend-a-new-gen-ai-gadget-is-the-most-depressing-weve-seen-so-far.html

NeurIPS. (n.d.). *2024 Conference*. https://neurips.cc/

Ng, A. (n.d.). *Letters from Andrew Ng | The Batch*. DeepLearningAI. https://www.deeplearning.ai/the-batch/tag/letters/

Nicioli, T. (2024, December 18). *AI chatbots are becoming popular for therapy. Here's what mental health experts say about them*. CNN. https://www.cnn.com/2024/12/18/health/chatbot-ai-therapy-risks-wellness/index.html

Nield, D. (2024, July 5). How to spot an AI-generated video. *Popular Science*. https://www.popsci.com/diy/how-to-spot-ai-generated-video/

Nietzel, M. (2022, July 29). Meet the world's most influential women engineers. *Forbes*. https://www.forbes.com/sites/michaeltnietzel/2021/07/03/meet-the-worlds-most-influential-women-engineers/?sh=1e4d636f34c0

Nonprofit Apps. (2023, June 22). *Generative Artificial Intelligence for Nonprofits: A Comprehensive guide*. https://nonprofit-apps.com/generative-artificial-intelligence-for-nonprofits-a-comprehensive-guide/

O'Brien, M., & Parvini, S. (2024, December 30). *In 2024, artificial intelligence was all about putting AI tools to work*. AP News. https://apnews.com/article/ai-artificial-intelligence-0b6ab89193265c3f60f382bae9bbabc9

O'Donnell, J. (2024, September 17). Why OpenAI's new model is such a big deal. *MIT Technology Review*. https://www.technologyreview.com/2024/09/17/1104004/why-openais-new-model-is-such-a-big-deal/

Office of the Governor. (2024, January 10). *Tennessee First in the Nation to Address AI Impact on Music Industry* [Press release]. https://www.tn.gov/governor/news/2024/1/10/tennessee-first-in-the-nation-to-address-ai-impact-on-music-industry.html

O'Flaherty, K. (2024, June 4). AI is your coworker now. Can you trust it? *WIRED*. https://www.wired.com/story/ai-workplace-privacy-security/

OpenAI. (2025, January 31). *OpenAI o3-mini* [Press release]. https://openai.com/index/openai-o3-mini/

*OpenAI finalizes "o3 mini" reasoning AI model version, to launch it soon.* (2025, January 17). Reuters. https://www.reuters.com/technology/artificial-intelligence/openai-finalizes-o3-mini-reasoning-ai-model-version-launch-it-soon-2025-01-17/

Ortiz, S. (2024, December 13). *The best AI chatbots of 2024: ChatGPT, Copilot, and notable alternatives.* ZDNET. https://www.zdnet.com/article/best-ai-chatbot/

Paradis, T. (2024a, September 29). *Sam Altman says learning AI will keep humans employed. Here's why else the robots might not take your job.* Business Insider. https://www.businessinsider.com/ai-wont-take-as-many-jobs-as-feared-altman-2024-9

Paradis, T. (2024b, December 22). *The AI job market is set to snowball in 2025.* Business Insider. https://www.businessinsider.com/ai-job-market-to-grow-2025-employers-hiring-talent-tech-2024-12

Parsons, A. (2022, October 18). *The Content Authenticity Initiative announces major partnerships with Leica and Nikon at MAX 2022 | Adobe Blog.* https://blog.adobe.com/en/publish/2022/10/18/major-steps-forward-cai-partnerships-leica-nikon-new-content-credentials-features-photoshop-beyond-max-2022

Parsons, A. (2024, January 26). *Seizing the moment and driving adoption for Content Credentials in 2024 | Adobe Blog.* https://blog.adobe.com/en/publish/2024/01/26/seizing-moment-content-credentials-in-2024

*Partnership on AI - Home.* (n.d.). Partnership on AI. https://partnershiponai.org/

payman89. (2023). *The nudity filters on V6 are a lot more relaxed [Online forum post].* Reddit. https://old.reddit.com/r/midjourney/comments/18w19tb/the_nudity_filters_on_v6_are_a_lot_more_relaxed/

Peters, J. (2024, December 3). Amazon announces its own set of Nova AI models. *The Verge.* https://www.theverge.com/2024/12/3/24312260/amazon-nova-foundation-ai-models-anthropic

Peterson, J. (2024, August 12). *How to identify AI-Generated Speech.* Lifehacker. https://lifehacker.com/tech/how-to-identify-ai-generated-speech

Pierce, K. (2023, March 8). Female Linguists who Changed the World. *Language Academia.* https://www.languageacademia.com/post/female-linguists-who-changed-the-world

Pillay, T. (2024, September 5). Kristen DiCerbo, Chief Learning Officer, Khan Academy. *TIME.* https://time.com/7012801/kristen-dicerbo/

PluralSight. (n.d.). *Online courses, learning paths, and certifications.* https://www.pluralsight.com/

Pratap, A. (2025, February 7). *AI drug discovery start-up wins funding.* Chemical & Engineering News. https://cen.acs.org/business/informatics/AI-drug-discovery-start Manas-secures/103/i3

*Projects & tools.* (n.d.). Berkman Klein Center. https://cyber.harvard.edu/projects-tools

PromptHub. (n.d.). *PromptHub: AI Prompt Management for teams.* https://www.prompthub.us/

Promptmetheus. (n.d.). *PromptMetheus: Prompt Engineering IDE.* https://promptmetheus.com/

Quora. (2024, October 3). Departments and industries that benefit from AI video generation. *Forbes*. https://www.forbes.com/sites/quora/2024/10/03/departments-and-industries-that-benefit-from-ai-video-generation/

Rainie, L., Anderson, J., & Imagining the Digital Future Center. (2024). Experts imagine the impact of artificial intelligence by 2040. In *Imagining the Digital Future Center*. https://imaginingthedigitalfuture.org/wp-content/uploads/2024/02/AI2040-FINAL-White-Paper-2-2.29.24.pdf

Raj, A. (2023, October). *Some of the weirdest generative AI use cases just got weirder*. Tech Wire Asia. https://techwireasia.com/2023/10/what-are-the-weirdest-generative-ai-use-cases/

Raj J, A. S. (2024). GenAI and the future of education and research. *SSRN Electronic Journal*. https://doi.org/10.2139/ssrn.4686338

Rajvanshi, A. (2024, September 5). India is emerging as a key player in the global AI race. *TIME*. https://time.com/7018294/india-ai-artificial-intelligence-ambani/

Readio. (2024, September 16). Friend AI: the wearable tech designed to keep you company. *Medium*. https://medium.com/@dhananjaymohan67/friend-ai-the-wearable-tech-designed-to-keep-you-company-0a35b21c3cf1

*Real or Fake: the AI game*. (n.d.). Render. https://real-or-fake-the-ai-game.onrender.com/

Rebelo, M. (2024, September 17). *The 9 best AI video generators in 2024*. Zapier. https://zapier.com/blog/best-ai-video-generator/

Ren, H., Sun, K., Zhao, F., & Zhu, X. (2024). Dunhuang murals image restoration method based on generative adversarial network. *Heritage Science*, *12*(1), 39. https://doi.org/10.1186/s40494-024-01159-8

*Rest of World - Reporting Global Tech Stories*. (n.d.). Rest of World. https://restofworld.org/

Reuters. (2024a, October 25). *Universal Music release AI-powered Spanish version of Brenda Lee's hit song*. https://www.reuters.com/technology/artificial-intelligence/universal-music-release-ai-powered-spanish-version-brenda-lees-hit-song-2024-10-25/

Reuters. (2024b, December 20). *OpenAI unveils "o3" reasoning AI models in test phase*. https://www.reuters.com/technology/artificial-intelligence/openai-unveils-o3-reasoning-ai-models-test-phase-2024-12-20

Robins-Early, N. (2024, May 10). CEO of world's biggest ad firm targeted by deepfake scam. *The Guardian*. https://www.theguardian.com/technology/article/2024/may/10/ceo-wpp-deepfake-scam

Robison, K. (2024, December 20). OpenAI teases new reasoning model—but don't expect to try it soon. *The Verge*. https://www.theverge.com/2024/12/20/24326036/openai-o1-o2-o3-reasoning-model-testing

Romero, A. (2024, February 16). OpenAI Sora: One step away from the matrix. *The Algorithmic Bridge*. https://www.thealgorithmicbridge.com/p/openai-sora-one-step-away-from-the

Rosselle, E. (2022, October 19). *Floating solar panels in Japan use generative design*. Autodesk. https://www.autodesk.com/design-make/articles/floating-solar

Roth, E. (2025, January 23). Perplexity now has a mobile assistant on Android. *The Verge*. https://www.theverge.com/2025/1/23/24350488/perplexity-ai-mobile-assistant-android

Sala, A. (2024, May 27). *AI watermarking: A watershed for multimedia authenticity*.

International Telecommunication Union (ITU). https://www.itu.int/hub/2024/05/ai-watermarking-a-watershed-for-multimedia-authenticity/

Scao, T. L., & Fan, A. (2023). A 176B-Parameter Open-Access Multilingual Language Model. *arXiv*. https://arxiv.org/pdf/2211.05100

Schrader, A. (2023, September 26). Another A.I.-Generated artwork was denied copyright protection, adding a new knot to the complexities of creative ownership. *Artnet News*. https://news.artnet.com/art-world/ai-art-copyright-2367590

Schreiber, M. (2024, March 25). *Why large language models like ChatGPT treat Black- and White-Sounding names differently*. Stanford HAI. https://hai.stanford.edu/news/why-large-language-models-chatgpt-treat-black-and-white-sounding-names-differently

Scribbr. (n.d.). *Free AI Detector*. https://www.scribbr.com/ai-detector/

Sensity. (n.d.). *All-In-One Deepfake Detection*. https://sensity.ai/

Sharma, A., Ajadi, S., & Beavor, A. (n.d.). Artificial Intelligence and Start-Ups in Low- and Middle-Income Countries: Progress, Promises and Perils. In *GSMA*. https://www.gsma.com/solutions-and-impact/connectivity-for-good/mobile-for-development/wp-content/uploads/2020/10/Artificial-Intelligence-and-Start-Ups-in-Low-and-Middle-Income-Countries-Progress-Promises-Perils-Final.pdf

Sharma, G. (2023, November 25). *3 ways to detect AI generated voice or audio - gadgets to use*. Gadgets to Use. https://gadgetstouse.com/blog/2023/11/24/detect-ai-generated-voice-audio/

Sharma, S. (2024, December 30). Inside the AI agent revolution: How data-driven automation transformed the enterprise in 2024. *VentureBeat*. https://venturebeat.com/data-infrastructure/unlocking-value-from-data-how-ai-agents-conquered-2024/

Shellhorn, B. (2024, October 14). *AI Wearables: The unusual and thrilling future of marketing*. Aquent Talent. https://aquenttalent.com/blog/ai-wearables-the-unusual-and-thrilling-future-of-marketing

Shrivastava, R. (2024, November 5). The prompt: Perplexity's erroneous AI election info. *Forbes*. https://www.forbes.com/sites/rashishrivastava/2024/11/05/the-prompt-perplexitys-erroneous-ai-election-info/

Shutterstock. (2023, July 11). *Shutterstock Expands Partnership with OpenAI, Signs New Six-Year Agreement to Provide High-Quality Training Data* [Press release]. https://investor.shutterstock.com/news-releases/news-release-details/shutterstock-expands-partnership-openai-signs-new-six-year

Siemens. (n.d.). *Unlocking the power of Generative AI: Siemens industrial Copilot*. https://www.siemens.com/global/en/company/insights/unlocking-the-power-of-generative-ai-siemens-industrial-copilot.html

Singla, A., Sukharevsky, A., Yee, L., & Chui, M. (2024, May 30). *The state of AI in early 2024: Gen AI adoption spikes and starts to generate value*. McKinsey & Company. https://www.mckinsey.com/capabilities/quantumblack/our-insights/the-state-of-ai

Sipes, E. (2023, November 11). *Uncover the Magic of AI Tome: your guide to new tech trends*. ParanoidPark. https://paranoidpark.co.uk/ai-tome/

Smith, B. (2024, July 30). *Protecting the public from abusive AI-generated content*. Microsoft on the Issues. https://blogs.microsoft.com/on-the-issues/2024/07/30/protecting-the-public-from-abusive-ai-generated-content/

Smith, C. S. (2025, January 7). *Entering the artificial General intelligence spectrum in 2025.* Forbes. https://www.forbes.com/sites/craigsmith/2025/01/07/entering-the-artificial-general-intelligence-spectrum-in-2025/

Sophia, D.M. (2025, February 11). Shopify rings in strong holiday sales, profit outlook underwhelms. *Reuters.* https://www.reuters.com/business/retail-consumer/shopify-beats-holiday-quarter-revenue-estimates-higher-consumer-spending-2025-02-11/

Spicer, N. (2021, December 9). *10 female engineers who changed our world.* WeTheParents. https://wetheparents.org/inspiring-engineering-women

Springer Nature. (2019, April 2). *Springer Nature publishes its first machine-generated book* [Press release]. https://www.springer.com/gp/about-springer/media/press-releases/corporate/springer-nature-machine-generated-book/16590126

Springer Nature. (2023, October 18). *Springer Nature and authors successfully use generative AI to publish academic book* [Press release]. https://group.springernature.com/gp/group/media/press-releases/first-ai-generated-book/26189712

Sravani. (2024, April 24). *Rabbit R1 vs AI Pin: Detailed Comparison in 2024.* GeeksforGeeks. https://www.geeksforgeeks.org/rabbit-r1-vs-ai-pin-detailed-comparison/

Sweet, J. (2024, June 19). *Harnessing the power of GenAI for the energy transition.* World Economic Forum. https://www.weforum.org/stories/2024/06/harness-power-generative-ai-energy-transition/

Talagala, N. (2024, December 30). Five AI trends to expect in 2025: Beyond ChatGPT and Friends. *Forbes.* https://www.forbes.com/sites/nishatalagala/2024/12/30/five-ai-trends-to-expect-in-2025-beyond-chatgpt-and-friends/

Telpizov, R. (2024, October 7). How AI tools helped my company stand out in a crowded market. *Entrepreneur.* https://www.entrepreneur.com/growing-a-business/how-ai-tools-helped-my-company-stand-out-in-a-crowded-market/480180

Thaler, S. (2024, May 10). CEO of WPP, world's biggest advertising agency, falls victim to elaborate deepfake scam. *New York Post.* https://nypost.com/2024/05/10/business/ceo-of-wpp-falls-victim-to-deepfake-scam/?utm_source=chatgpt.com

Thapa, R. (2024, April 9). *Developing AI for development.* World Bank. https://accountability.worldbank.org/en/news/2024/Developing-AI-for-development

Thompson Reuters. (n.d.). *The legal AI you've been waiting for: What can CoCounsel do?* https://casetext.com/cocounsel/

Timonera, K. (2024, September 6). *The future of Generative AI: 8 predictions to watch.* eWEEK. https://www.eweek.com/artificial-intelligence/future-of-generative-ai/

Townsend, C. (2024, November 26). How to detect AI-generated text. *Mashable.* https://mashable.com/article/how-to-identify-ai-generated-text

Tuchman, R. (2024, June 13). This Nurse-Turned-Entrepreneur saw the needs of underserved communities firsthand. Now, his company uses AI to help them. *Entrepreneur.* https://www.entrepreneur.com/growing-a-business/nurse-turned-entrepreneur-uses-ai-to-help-underserved/474760

Turner, M. (2024, October 3). Modified Meta AI glasses used to 'reveal anyone's personal info' in Seconds just by looking at them. *The Irish Sun*. https://www.thesun.ie/tech/13939493/meta-ai-ray-ban-glasses-reveal-personal-information/

Twarogal, P., & Dobosz, M. (2024, December 9). *Generative AI—the Ultimate overview: use cases, models, and tools*. Neontri. https://neontri.com/blog/generative-ai-overview/

UNHCR. (2024). Global Trends. In *UNHCR - the UN Refugee Agency*. https://www.unhcr.org/global-trends

USAFacts. (2024). Which US cities have the largest homeless populations? *USAFacts*. https://usafacts.org/articles/which-cities-in-the-us-have-the-most-homelessness/

*Use case: Reinforcement Learning for Robotics*. (n.d.). NVIDIA. https://www.nvidia.com/en-us/use-cases/reinforcement-learning/

Vakili, M. G., et al. (2024). Quantum Computing-Enhanced Algorithm unveils novel inhibitors for KRAS. *arXiv.org*. https://arxiv.org/abs/2402.08210

Valerie [Valerie]. (2023, October 2). AI wearables: What's new? *Medium*. https://medium.com/dare-to-be-better/ai-wearables-the-next-big-thing-a84ad82e4132

Weatherbed, J. (2024, October 25). Adobe execs say artists need to embrace AI or get left behind. *The Verge*. https://www.theverge.com/2024/10/25/24278715/adobe-artists-embrace-generative-ai-creative-community

Weatherbed, J. (2025, February 18). Elon Musk's xAI adds 'Big Brain' reasoning to Grok-3. *The Verge*. https://www.theverge.com/news/614218/elon-musk-xai-big-brain-reasoning-grok-3

White, J. B. (2024, September 17). *Gavin Newsom signs election "deepfake" ban in rebuke to Elon Musk*. Politico. https://www.politico.com/news/2024/09/17/newsom-signs-election-deepfake-ban-00179557

Wiggers, K. (2024, April 21). Women in AI: Anna Korhonen studies the intersection between linguistics and AI. *TechCrunch*. https://techcrunch.com/2024/04/21/women-in-ai-anna-korhonen-studies-the-intersection-between-linguistics-and-ai/

Williams, S. (2024, February 26). AI and Artists' IP: Exploring Copyright Infringement Allegations in Andersen v. Stability AI Ltd. - Center for Art Law. *Center for Art Law*. https://itsartlaw.org/2024/02/26/artificial-intelligence-and-artists-intellectual-property-unpacking-copyright-infringement-allegations-in-andersen-v-stability-ai-ltd/

Wilser, J. (2024, October 30). A chatbot for farmers. *TIME*. https://time.com/7094874/farmerline-darli-ai/

Winship, L. (2024, October 29). Small step or a giant leap? What AI means for the dance world. *The Guardian*. https://www.theguardian.com/stage/2024/oct/29/small-step-or-a-giant-leap-what-ai-means-for-the-dance-world

Wu, R. (2024, November 26). 5 ways AI can Accelerate your entrepreneurial journey. *Entrepreneur*. https://www.entrepreneur.com/science-technology/5-ways-ai-can-accelerate-your-entrepreneurial-journey/482659

Made in the USA
Las Vegas, NV
25 March 2025

20121419R00095